Your
EXAMPLE

"'Imitate me, just as I also imitate Christ' (1 Cor. 11:1). *Your Example* is a worthwhile read for all who are trusting in the Lord Jesus Christ, seeking to make progress in their walk with the Lord, and living out a godly life. Well-researched and written, each page is filled with Scripture, which makes for an edifying and challenging read as you seek to walk in a manner worthy of the calling to which you have been called."

—Pastor Stuart Davis
Trinity Road Chapel

"Are you an exemplary Christian? Have you stopped to consider what an influence you can have over other people? What are the values that you most cherish that cause you to be an example? Have you thought about how much the Bible calls Christians to be exemplary? People in Rome may do as the Romans do, but people in Christ should do as Christ would do. The apostle John addresses his readers with these all-important words: 'Beloved, do not imitate what is evil, but what is good' (3 John 11). The Bible calls us to heed its good examples and shun the bad ones. Join Terence Crosby as he traces such themes and examples through the Old and New Testaments, illustrating and applying them to modern readers."

—Jim Holmes
Publishing Consultant, Taylors, SC

"This edifying little book reminds us of the power of personal example, a theme which is too often neglected today. Both positive and negative role models are highlighted from Scripture, and we see that this was a key element of apostolic exhortation. We are encouraged to take heed ourselves and to follow this pattern as we seek to teach and preach the Scriptures. More than that, we are reminded that we are to be a good example to others. Warmly commended!"

—Bill James
Principal, London Seminary

Your EXAMPLE

A STUDY OF THE NEW TESTAMENT DOCTRINE OF IMITATION

Terence Crosby

AMBASSADOR INTERNATIONAL

GREENVILLE, SOUTH CAROLINA & BELFAST, NORTHERN IRELAND

www.ambassador-international.com

Your Example
A Study of the New Testament Doctrine of Imitation
©2025 by Terence Crosby
All rights reserved

ISBN: 978-1-64960-620-4, hardcover
ISBN: 978-1-64960-877-2, paperback
eISBN: 978-1-64960-671-6

Cover Design by Karen Slayne
Interior Typesetting by Dentelle Design
Edited by Valerie Coffman

Unless otherwise marked, Scripture taken from the New King James Version®. Copyright © 1982 by Thomas Nelson. Used by permission. All rights reserved.

Scripture quotations marked NIV taken from The Holy Bible, New International Version®, NIV®. Copyright © 1973, 1978, 1984, 2011 by Biblica, Inc. Used with permission of Zondervan. All rights reserved worldwide. www.zondervan.com

Titles may be purchased in bulk for education, business, fundraising, or sales promotional use. For information, please email sales@emeraldhouse.com.

AMBASSADOR INTERNATIONAL
Emerald House
411 University Ridge, Suite B14
Greenville, SC 29601
United States
www.ambassador-international.com

AMBASSADOR BOOKS
The Mount
2 Woodstock Link
Belfast, BT6 8DD
Northern Ireland, United Kingdom
www.ambassadormedia.co.uk

The colophon is a trademark of Ambassador, a Christian publishing company.

"This edifying little book reminds us of the power of personal example, a theme which is too often neglected today. Both positive and negative role models are highlighted from Scripture, and we see that this was a key element of apostolic exhortation. We are encouraged to take heed ourselves and to follow this pattern as we seek to teach and preach the Scriptures. More than that, we are reminded that we are to be a good example to others. Warmly commended!"

—Bill James
Principal, London Seminary

In memory of Gordon Buchanan (1912-2001)

A Christ-like Bible class leader and a model of godliness

TABLE OF CONTENTS

AUTHOR'S NOTE

HOW EASILY ONE THING LEADS to another! When I was studying for my first degree, one of my special authors was the Latin historian Livy, in particular the first three books of his massive 142-book history of Rome, *Ab Urbe Condita*. One of my essays dealt with the way in which he used particular words to emphasize the stated aim of his preface to provide examples of behavior to be avoided or followed. Later, in the thesis for my doctorate, I was able to expand the principles of that short essay to cover all thirty-five of Livy's surviving books.

As an appendix, I extended my studies to see how other classical historians treated the subject of exemplification. *Your Example* represents a further expansion of these studies to cover the presentation of examples in the New Testament, compiled during the period not long after Livy had been writing. An abbreviated form of some of the material in this volume appeared in a couple of short chapters of my *Opening Up 2 & 3 John*, published by Day One Publications in 2006. I am grateful to Mark Roberts, managing director of Day One, for indicating in writing that he has no problem with the overlap of some material, which now appears here in its original intended and extended form.

How easily one thing leads to another! The same thing could be said about the whole idea of examples. In the first place, "your example" means the example set by another person for you to follow or avoid. But that is only the start of the process. In the second place, "your example" becomes the example set by you for others to follow or avoid. The title of this book has a double meaning! The following chapters trace the idea of exemplification in the New Testament from its context in the early days of the Roman Empire to specific areas of doctrine and practice relevant to the lives of every Christian believer today. May we all copy the best examples and, in so doing, provide the best examples for others to copy!

Chapter 1
THE NEW TESTAMENT IN
THE ROMAN WORLD

"WHEN IN ROME, DO AS the Romans do" may be one of the world's famous sayings; but for the most part, it is far from being good advice for the Christian to follow. The teaching of the apostles, inspired by the Holy Spirit of God, was quite the opposite. Many today may attempt to fudge the issue, but the command of the apostle Paul was uncompromisingly clear-cut: "This I say, therefore, and testify in the Lord, that you should no longer walk as the rest of the Gentiles walk" (Eph. 4:17). The apostle Peter was no less forthright: "We have spent enough of our past lifetime in doing the will of the Gentiles—when we walked in lewdness, lusts, drunkenness, revelries, drinking parties, and abominable idolatries" (1 Peter 4:3). The facts of being "in the world" (John 17:11) and being sent by Christ "into the world" (John 17:18) must be balanced by the command not to "be conformed to this world" (Rom. 12:2); the obedient Christian cannot comply with the advice "When in the world, do as the world does." A higher principle is called for, and that is the main thrust of the following chapters.

Perhaps the point is most clear replacing the world's saying with something like "When in Christ, do as Christ does" or "When in Christ, do as Christians should do." The Christian has not only a physical address in the world, but also a spiritual address in Christ. In both Philippians 1:1 and Colossians 1:2, it is this spiritual address which is placed first and which is of far greater importance. The behavior of Paul's friend Onesiphorus in Rome is a good illustration of a man who understood this and who consequently got his priorities right. When in Rome, Onesiphorus refused to do as the Romans do but took the unfashionable but Christlike step (see Matt. 25:36) of searching Rome for the imprisoned and lonely apostle, who had, for the most part, been deserted as his execution approached. In Paul's own words, "When he arrived in Rome, he sought me out very zealously and found me" (2 Tim. 1:17). The motto of Onesiphorus could well have been "When in Rome, do as Christ does."

Sadly, this has not always been the approach taken by the Christian Church. If its leaders had remained mindful of these principles, they surely would never have adopted various pagan practices, which were totally unnecessary and inappropriate to the Christian faith. Pagan Roman religion, for example, had a system of priests headed up by a high priest, the *pontifex maximus*; in the time of the emperors, this title was assumed by the emperor himself. Within only a few centuries, ecclesiastical Rome had taken over this title and role. The result was the establishment of its own Pontificate with its own high priest, the Pope, and the development of what is now known as "the Church of Rome."[1] The principle "when in Rome, do as the Romans do" was in disastrous operation.

This fact would probably not have been admitted in such terms. However, behind such corruptions of the Christian faith, there was, indeed, a plausible argument, described as "the spoiling of the Egyptians" and based upon the account of the Exodus; the Children of Israel left Egypt carrying with them silver, gold, and clothing plundered from the Egyptians (Exod. 11:2; 12:35, 36), who were glad to see the back of them following the disasters of the first Passover. This event was used as a scriptural precedent for adopting, converting, and "Christianizing" any pagan idea or practice which could be put to Christian use. The closest modern equivalent to this argument is probably the question, "Why should the devil have all the best tunes?" It does not take much discernment to see that such an approach, though more guarded than the broader "When in Rome, do as the Romans do" principle, was still fraught with danger; it can be just as dangerous in our own generation.

---

1   Loraine Boettner, *Roman Catholicism* (London, Banner of Truth, 1966), 166-7.

However, it is also obvious that there were aspects of the Roman world which were not inappropriate to the Christian faith. The very concept of "doing as somebody else does" (in a good and moral sense) was extremely popular in the Roman world at the time of the New Testament. It was one aspect of contemporary thought which lent itself to Christian usage and which could be adopted in the New Testament under the guidance of the Holy Spirit without there being any question of compromise. As it is never good practice to consider individual topics in glorious isolation, the aim of this chapter is to set the scene and to paint in the wider background before proceeding to a detailed examination of this one specific subject.

The original force and context of the Greek New Testament can be easily masked by several factors—the passage of time (some two thousand years), the use of translations in foreign languages (including English), and—at least, for those of us who live in the West—the influence of Western thought patterns upon our minds. It does us no harm to have some reminder of the historical, political, social, and literary climates which prevailed in the time of our Savior and in the period immediately following while the New Testament was being written.

THE HISTORICAL SETTING

At the time in question, Rome ruled the known world. The world's greatest empire was at its height, and the first of the long line of Roman emperors had only recently appeared on the scene. God chose this particular time to upstage the world's great men by sending into the Roman-occupied land of Judea His only-begotten Son, the King of kings, to proclaim and establish His greater and eternal kingdom!

We meet most of the early emperors in the New Testament, starting in the Gospels with the very first, Augustus (63 BC-AD 14), through whose decree the location of our Savior's birth was, humanly speaking, determined (Luke 2:1). In AD 14, Augustus was succeeded by Tiberius (42 BC-AD 37) in the fifteenth year of whose reign the ministry of John the Baptist began (Luke 3:1). Without doubt, it was the likeness and inscription of Tiberius, as the current emperor, which was on the coin shown to Jesus by His questioners (Matt. 22:19ff). His response "render therefore to Caesar [namely Tiberius] the things that are Caesar's, and to God the things that are God's" (Matt. 22:21) was yet another caution against the principle, "When in the Roman world, do as the Romans do." Subsequent events were to demonstrate that His caution had fallen upon deaf ears because it was this ungodly principle which still controlled the actions not only of the Roman governor, Pontius Pilate, but also of the Jewish chief priests. Pilate, pressured by the Jewish crowd, chose to authorize the crucifixion of the Son of God, rather than to risk losing his friendship with Tiberius by daring to release one accused of speaking against Tiberius (John 19:12); the chief priests also publicly rejected King Jesus in favor of the Emperor Tiberius (John 19:15).

The book of Acts does not mention Tiberius in his last years or the short reign of Caligula (AD 12-41), who succeeded him in AD 37, but does refer to the reigns of Claudius (10 BC-AD 54) and Nero (AD 37-68), which commenced in AD 41 and 54 respectively. In the time of Claudius, there was a widespread famine, which resulted in Christian relief work (Acts 11:28-29). Claudius was also responsible for expelling all Jews from Rome (Acts 18:2). When on trial, the apostle Paul appealed to the judgment of the Emperor Nero (Acts 25:10-11); and there were saints in Nero's household (Phil. 4:22). This was the calm before the storm. Claudius had merely expelled the Jews from Rome, but Nero was soon to inflict terrible persecution upon the Christians in Rome. Imminent persecution also formed the background to Peter's first epistle, addressed to believers scattered throughout the Roman Empire; but they were still to be subject to the emperor (Nero at the time of writing), rendering to God the fear due to Him and to Caesar the honor due to him (1 Pet. 2:13, 17).

Following Nero's suicide in AD 68, the emperors Galba, Otho, and Vitellius followed and departed in very quick succession. Stability returned in the reign of Vespasian (AD 69-77), but not for the Jews. One year into Vespasian's reign, the future emperor Titus presided over the destruction of Jerusalem, as prophesied by our Savior (Luke 21:20-24), a final and terrible demonstration that the time of the New Testament cannot be properly understood without taking into account its context within the world of imperial Rome.

THE POLITICAL AND SOCIAL SETTING

Roman emperors played their part in the unfolding history of the New Testament but did so largely in the background and in ignorance. It was left to lesser officials to deal firsthand with the affairs of the provinces occupied by Rome. Luke names several provincial governors, beginning in his Gospel with Quirinius in Syria (Luke 2:2) and Pontius Pilate in Judea (Luke 3:1; 13:1); in Acts 24-26, he includes accounts of the apostle Paul's dealings with Felix and Porcius Festus, later governors of Judea. Others fulfilling a governing role in the time of Paul's missionary journeys were Sergius Paulus, converted while proconsul of Cyprus (Acts 13:7, 12) and Gallio, proconsul of Achaia while Paul was at Corinth (Acts 18:12-17). Rome's authority and rule was maintained by its military might, and no reader of the New Testament should be surprised to find marching regularly across its pages Roman soldiers and commanding officers holding ranks such as military tribune or centurion. The attempted murder of Paul in Jerusalem led to military intervention by the "commander of the garrison," "soldiers and centurions" (Acts 21:31-32).

"When in the Roman world, use Roman illustrations" is a principle regularly applied in Paul's epistles. Some of his most striking illustrations have a military flavor; a Roman soldier in full armor and carrying a shield as big as a door was Paul's model for illustrating a good soldier of Jesus Christ wearing "the whole armor of God" (Eph. 6:13-17). His readers would also have been familiar with the Roman practice of awarding a victory-parade known as a "triumph" to a victorious general. Paul twice used this as a picture of the victory-celebrations of the Lord Jesus Christ, followed in the procession by His victorious army (2 Cor. 2:14) and His defeated spiritual enemies (Col. 2:15).

The pervading influence of Roman society is also to be found in Paul's epistles. Greek and Roman institutions of education, adoption, and slavery are used to illustrate various spiritual truths. For example, to explain the role of the Jewish law, Paul utilized the classical role of the slave who acted as a child's disciplinary escort to school. Just as the child, reaching maturity, no longer needed to be under an escort, so the believer, having come to faith in Christ, is no longer under the dominion of the law (Gal. 3:23-25). In a similar way, Paul took illustrations from various aspects of the Greek athletic games, particularly the disciplines of running and boxing and the awards presented to victorious athletes. On a personal level, his Roman citizenship stood him in great stead during his missionary journeys, and he was not slow to avail himself of its privileges (Acts 16:37-38; 22:25-29).

Another unavoidable aspect of New Testament times was false belief. Paul had to grapple not only with a Judaism corrupted by the rejection of the Messiah but also with a world dominated by the religious, mythical, and philosophical ideas of the Greeks and Romans. In Lystra, Barnabas and Paul were mistaken for Zeus/Jupiter (king of the pagan gods and god of the sky and weather) and Hermes/Mercury (messenger of the gods) respectively and had to resist being worshipped (Acts 14:11-18). At Ephesus, Paul offended the worshippers of Artemis/Diana (goddess of hunting), provoking a riot (Acts 19:23ff). In Athens, he could not help observing shrines to numerous pagan deities (Acts 17:23) and also encountered Epicureans and Stoics, representatives of the two main schools of philosophy (Acts 17:18). Epicureanism, a pursuit of happiness and contentment, in time developed into extravagant pleasure-seeking, while Stoicism, an attempt to come to terms with life as it is, was to gain the reputation of being a grim "grin and bear it" philosophy. Following his shipwreck as a prisoner bound for Rome, Paul completed his voyage on a ship with the twin brothers Castor and Pollux (patrons of sailors) as its figurehead (Acts 28:11).

Reaching Rome itself was Paul's great ambition (Acts 19:21; Rom. 1:10-13; 15:23-29) and God's will for him (Acts 23:11). Fittingly, Acts concludes on the high note of Paul entering the city and freely teaching the truth of the Gospel in the very center of pagan religion and of the Roman Empire (Acts 28:30-31).

THE LITERARY SETTING

In addition to drawing upon illustrations from the Roman world in which he lived, the apostle Paul, as an educated man, was at ease quoting occasionally from Greek authors. His sermon in the Areopagus at Athens appropriately included quotations from Epimenides of Crete and from Aratus, the author of an astronomical poem (Acts 17:28). When Paul wrote to Titus, who was based in

Crete, he quoted Epimenides' unflattering description of his own countrymen: "Cretans are always liars, evil beasts, lazy gluttons" (Titus 1:12). Paul also lifted the proverb, "Evil company corrupts good habits" (1 Cor. 15:33) from "Thais," a comedy by the Athenian comedy-writer Menander (342/1-293/89 BC). The New Testament itself is primarily a complete and unified work conceived and inspired in its entirety by God the Holy Spirit. On a human level, it is also a remarkably preserved compendium of Greek literature penned by Jewish authors in a freer and more common form of the great classical language, Greek. Its literary format is distinct from that of the Old Testament but typical of various forms of contemporary classical literature.

The four Gospels can be described as biographical monographs. Various writers popularized this format in the Latin language. Cornelius Nepos (c. 99-24 BC) wrote short lives of famous men, such as generals, historians, kings, poets and, perhaps, orators. Suetonius (born c. AD 69) wrote biographies of the first twelve Caesars from Julius Caesar to Domitian (AD 51-96). Tacitus (born c. AD 56) published in AD 98 a life of Agricola, governor of Britain. Writing in Greek, Plutarch (born before AD 50 and still alive in AD 120) produced numerous biographies of famous Greeks and Romans. It was in this context that the Gospels were written; but here, instead of reading about mere generals, emperors, kings, governors, and orators, we observe the kingdom of One prophesied to be "Ruler" of Israel (Matt. 2:6). We hear the preaching of One Who spoke more powerfully than any orator (John 7:46) and follow the life of the Captain of our salvation (Heb. 2:10), Who is no less than "KING OF KINGS AND LORD OF LORDS" (Rev. 19:16).

Luke's Gospel and its sequel, the Acts of the Apostles, can also be regarded as a pair of historical monographs, such as had come from the pen of the Latin author Sallust (86-35 BC). He had written briefly concerning two wars, as had Julius Caesar (100-44 BC), the latter at greater length and including an account of his invasion of Britain (55 and 54 BC). Luke and Acts deal with a far nobler theme—that of spiritual warfare, the defeat of Satan at Calvary's cross, the invasion and turning upside down of the world with the Gospel, and the proclamation of Jesus as another King superior to the current Emperor Claudius (Acts 17:6-7). To enliven their narratives, classical historians usually composed long political and battle speeches, sometimes greatly embellished, to place into the mouths of their heroes. In contrast, the Gospels and Acts naturally contain the teaching of the Lord Jesus Christ and of the apostles, who preached Christ crucified without the gimmicks and flourishes of impressive oratory (1 Cor. 1:17, 23; 2:1-4).

In the absence of all the modern forms of communication, which we take for granted, the writing of letters was a prominent part of Roman life. The most famous surviving collections are the natural letters of Cicero (106-43 BC) and the more deliberate and stylistic letters of the Younger Pliny (AD c. 61-c. 112). Their letters cover not only items of news but also discuss a wide range of topics. In this, the New Testament epistles—both the official letters to churches and the personal letters to individuals (i.e. Timothy, Titus, and Philemon)—are not unusual, except that the news content and the topics covered are all firmly gospel-related, whether dealt with doctrinally, practically or, in the case of Revelation, prophetically. In accordance with classical procedure, the names of the writer and addressee come at the beginning of the New Testament epistles.

Having briefly set the New Testament in its historical, political, social, and literary contexts, it should now be possible to embark with greater understanding upon a consideration of a particular aspect which was characteristic of Roman thought in New Testament times and which linked historical fact to literature. This consisted of the moralistic quotation of good examples of behavior to follow and of bad examples to avoid, a practice which Roman authors had developed into a sophisticated literary device. This prominent and prevailing contemporary teaching method was taken up, under the direction of God the Holy Spirit, by the writers of the New Testament epistles. In closing this chapter, it is interesting to note that the English language derives all its words on this subject from classical roots: "mimic" and "type" come from the Greek language, "example," "specimen," "document," and "imitate" from Latin.

Chapter 2
TEACHING BY EXAMPLES
IN THE ROMAN WORLD

IN THE NOT-TOO-DISTANT PAST, THE teaching of history may well have centered on the linking of dates and events. Today, there is much more concentration upon causes and effects, motives, and trends. As a result, historical events are not treated as mere facts to learn but can be subjected to every kind of analysis. However, much less attention is paid to the moral lessons taught by history. Few pupils are encouraged to emulate the lives and morals of any particular historical characters. This has not always been the case as a consideration of the position taken by the Puritans shows clearly. According to George Swinnock (1627-1673), "Man is a creature that is led more by patterns than by precepts."[2] Thomas Brooks (1608-1680) expressed the same thought even more forcefully: "Example is

---

2   Isaac Thomas, *A Puritan Golden Treasury* (Edinburgh, Banner of Truth, 1977), 95-6.

the most powerful rhetoric."[3] The very same attitude was held in New Testament times, moral concerns being of no little interest in the days of Caesar Augustus when permissiveness had become a major worry to many in the Roman world.

THE USE OF EXAMPLES IN EDUCATION AND HISTORY

Teaching from the examples of the past held an important place in the education system of ancient Rome. This was of particular relevance in the teaching of rhetoric, since well-chosen examples cited during and especially at the end of speeches could carry great weight both in the political arena and in the law courts. Roman pupils studying rhetoric in New Testament times would have been familiar with books of "exempla," consisting of anecdotes arranged under various captions especially for the purposes of rhetoric. Well-known compilers of these were Cornelius Nepos (c. 99-c. 24 BC) and Valerius Maximus, who lived during the reign of Tiberius and whose work was probably published soon after AD 31, almost contemporaneous with the public ministry of the Lord Jesus Christ.

The examples chosen by Valerius Maximus came from Roman and Greek history, with a heavy emphasis placed upon the history of Rome. They were arranged in nine books and under nearly ninety different categories. These are far too numerous to be

---

3   Ibid.

listed here, but the following selection of moral categories affords a valuable insight into the perceived needs and concerns of the age in which our Savior ministered. A profitable and interesting exercise could be to arrange biblical examples under these headings used by Valerius Maximus:

> Treason; character; courage; endurance; self-confidence; constancy; moderation; self-control and continence; poverty; modesty; marital love; friendship; generosity; humanity and mercy; the thankful; the ungrateful; chastity; things said or done boldly/with dignity/wisely/artfully; strictness; justice; enthusiasm and diligence; idleness; old age; ambition for glory; extravagance and passion; cruelty; anger or hatred; greed; pride and lack of self-control; treachery; rashness; error; vengeance; cruel words and wicked deeds; uncommon deaths.[4]

While examples drawn from past history were a useful tool for Roman orators, they were regarded as valuable on a far wider scale. In the preface to his world history, written in Greek between about 60 and 30 BC, Diodorus Siculus remarked that it is good to be able to use mistakes as warning examples and to imitate past successes. This kind of statement was to be repeated in the prefaces and works of many Greek and Latin

---

4   Valerius Maximus, *Factorum et dictorum memorarbilium libri novem (Classic reprint)* (London.Forgotten Books, 2019).

historians right through to medieval times and especially in the twelfth century AD. For example, Tacitus (born AD 56) saw history as the recording of good and evil deeds to inspire or deter posterity.[5]

Clearest of all and closest to New Testament times was the statement in the preface to the massive 142-book history of Rome by the historian Livy, who lived either from 59 BC to AD 17 or from 64 BC to AD 12. Livy stressed to his readers in general and possibly to the Emperor Caesar Augustus in particular that, "What chiefly makes the study of history beneficial and fruitful is this, that you behold the lessons of every kind of experience [literally 'example'] as upon a famous monument; from these you may choose for yourself and for your state what to imitate, and mark for avoidance what is shameful in its conception and shameful in its result."[6] Among the striking aspects of this statement is the fact that even a pagan historian could speak of private and public life in the same breath, which is a far cry from these so-called enlightened days when the most immoral of men can hold public office and at the same time be praised for being good politicians. For our purposes, Livy's statement serves to underline the citing of examples as an important feature of the current literary climate at the time when the New Testament was being acted out and recorded. Though the concept of teaching

---

5   Cornelius Tacitus, *Annals III*, 65, in *Annals and Histories: Tacitus* (London, Everyman, 2009).

6   Stephen Usher, trans. *The Historians of Greece and Rome* (London, Methuen & Co, 1970), 167.

by examples was not a new one, the strong emphasis placed upon it was a feature of the times. The Old Testament provides a considerable contrast.

THE USE OF EXAMPLES IN THE OLD TESTAMENT

Key words such as "example" and "imitate" are notably absent from the Old Testament. But while there is little teaching by way of example, the idea is occasionally to be found in the form of warnings, as in the following few cases.

When the children of Israel had settled in the Promised Land, the tribes of Reuben, Gad, and half of Manasseh returned to their agreed territories on the east of the Jordan and erected a replica altar to serve as a monument. The remaining tribes misinterpreted this as an act of rebelliousness and sent messengers to remind them of fairly recent acts of faithlessness, which had resulted in the judgement of God. "What treachery is this that you have committed against the God of Israel, to turn away this day from following the LORD? . . . Is the iniquity of Peor not enough for us . . . but that you must turn away this day from following the Lord? . . . Did not Achan the son of Zerah commit a trespass in the accursed thing, and wrath fell on all the congregation of Israel?" (Josh. 22:16-20).

A messenger could be prepared not only with examples to quote, but with a defense in case examples were quoted against him. King David tried to hide his adulterous act with Bathsheba by plotting her husband Uriah's death in the front line of battle. Uriah died as planned, but so did several others. The messenger was prepared, unnecessarily as it turned out, for David to react angrily to the loss of life.

> "If it happens that the king's wrath rises, and he says to you: 'Why did you approach so near to the city when you fought? Did you not know that they would shoot from the wall? Who struck Abimelech the son of Jerubbesheth? Was it not a woman who cast a piece of a millstone on him from the wall, so that he died in Thebez? Why did you go near the wall?' then you shall say, 'Your servant Uriah the Hittite is dead also'" (2 Sam. 11:20-21).

Those in positions of power and authority could influence others for good or bad simply through the examples they were setting. This was strikingly illustrated in the Persian court. When Queen Vashti disobeyed a command of King Ahasuerus, his courtiers were all too aware that her example could encourage other women to despise their husbands (Esther 1:17); on the other hand, making an example of her by punishing her would persuade other women to honor their husbands (Esther 1:20). Similarly, in the days following the Jews' return from exile, Nehemiah used the notorious example of an otherwise-wise king to rebuke many who had intermarried with foreigners, "Did not Solomon king of Israel sin by these things? . . . pagan women caused even him to sin" (Neh. 13:26).

Heeding a warning example could be in one's best interests, as illustrated in the account of the three summonses sent by Ahaziah, a wicked king of Israel, to the prophet Elijah (2 Kings 1:9-15). The first two attempts were carried out in such a high-handed manner by Ahaziah's officers that on both occasions, fire fell from Heaven at the instigation of Elijah and killed the army captain together with his fifty men. Learning the lesson quickly, the third captain knelt before Elijah, cited the two warning examples, begged for mercy, and not only survived but also succeeded in getting Elijah to accompany him back to the king. Other instances of warning examples being set or going unheeded appear in the prophets Ezekiel (23:46-48) and Jeremiah (3:6-8), respectively. However, while teaching by examples is not absent from the Old Testament, it is certainly not a prominent feature. The New Testament is quite different.

THE USE OF EXAMPLES IN THE NEW TESTAMENT

The usual teaching method employed by the Lord Jesus Christ was the telling of parables (Matt. 13:34), but it was not His only method. The Parable of the Good Samaritan ends with the command, "Go and do likewise" (Luke 10:37), which gives the parable the practical application of being a good example to copy. When asked to give teaching concerning prayer, Jesus did so by means of an example or pattern of prayer (Luke 11:1-4). In the Sermon on the Mount, His teaching on charitable deeds, praying, and fasting included vivid descriptions of the publicity-seeking approach of hypocrites as examples to be avoided (Matt. 6:2, 5, 7, 16); with regard to the vain repetition of the heathen in prayer, He said, "Do not be like them" (Matt. 6:8). On other occasions, the Savior readily cited examples and precedents in order to make a point. It will be worth considering a few instances.

Christ's enemies were often the object of such teaching methods. When the Pharisees criticized the disciples for the unlawful act of eating heads of grain on the Sabbath, Christ referred to the occasion when David and his hungry men likewise unlawfully consumed the showbread reserved for the priests in the house of God (Matt. 12:2-4). Soon afterwards, to the same critics, He quoted Jonah in the fish as a type of His imminent burial in the earth and the repentance of the men of Nineveh, following the preaching of Jonah, as a condemnation of those who were refusing to repent at the preaching of One greater than Jonah (Matt. 12:38-41). Christ likewise exposed the chief priests and elders for their failure to follow the example of tax collectors and harlots, whom they had personally witnessed repenting and believing the preaching of John the Baptist (Matt. 21:31-32). Sadducees who tried to trick Christ on the subject of resurrection were answered by the example of Moses' statement that God was still the God of Abraham, Isaac, and Jacob, even though these were already physically dead at the time (Luke 20:37).

Examples were sometimes Christ's way of "hitting the nail on the head." His likening of Himself to prophets not accepted in their own countries was far too near the mark for His own countrymen. They proceeded to reject Him in the very same way when He underlined the fact by giving them the examples of Elijah being sent only to a foreign widow and Elisha cleansing only a foreign leper, rather than attending to the numerous widows and lepers in Israel (Luke 4:24-28). Some who were plotting to kill Christ on another occasion were exposed by the citation of Abraham's example; Abraham would never have tried to kill someone bringing him God's truth; their failure to follow Abraham's example showed that they were not the true children of Abraham they claimed to be (John 8:39-40). When His enemies condemned Him for healing the sick on the Sabbath, He only had to point to their own examples to expose their hypocrisy and silence them; they had no qualms about coming to the aid of their oxen and donkeys on the Sabbath, so what right had they to condemn Him for doing exactly the same for needy people (Luke 13:14-17; 14:3-6)?

Those who quoted to Him "the Galileans whose blood Pilate had mingled with their sacrifices" had the example thrown back at them together with that of the eighteen who had been crushed to death under the tower of Siloam. Both disasters were warnings of what the Romans would do to them all if they failed to repent (Luke 13:1-5). Likewise, Christ used examples from the time of Noah and Lot—"Remember Lot's wife" (Luke 17:32)—to warn His disciples to be prepared for momentous events to come (Luke 17:26-32). When they asked Him who was the greatest in the kingdom of Heaven, Jesus presented a little child as an example of the childlike attitude without which they would not even enter the kingdom of Heaven (Matt. 18:1-3). He twice commended the good example of Martha's sister Mary as a rebuke to others (Luke 10:41-42; John 12:3-8).

However, teaching by examples is not really a prominent feature of the four Gospels; only in John 13:15 (which will be considered in a later chapter) does a Greek noun meaning "pattern" or "example" appear in a moral sense. A related verb occurs in Matthew 1:19: Joseph, not yet understanding Mary's role in the imminent virgin birth, refused "to make her a public example."

When we come to the book of Acts, we find that exemplification is conspicuous by its almost total absence. There are only two exceptions. When the Jewish authorities were wondering what to do about the early Christians, the Pharisee Gamaliel advised caution. If the new movement was of human origin, it would collapse; and to support his case, he cited the abortive movements of Theudas and Judas of Galilee as examples (Acts 5:35-39). In the other instance, the tables were turned. Stephen was on trial before the Jewish authorities; but in his great address before his martyrdom, the authorities were on trial before God and open to the accusation of following their ancestors' example of resisting the Holy Spirit. Their fathers had persecuted and killed God's prophets, but they had gone one stage further and had actually executed God's Son, the promised Messiah (Acts 7:51-52).

In many respects, the book of Acts is descriptive, rather than prescriptive; and this is illustrated by the absence of specific examples for its readers to follow or avoid. Its main purpose is to tell us what God did through the apostles then, not to provide blueprints for believers to copy now. In some matters, it can be highly dangerous to imitate apostolic practice, as the sons of Sceva discovered to their cost when they attempted to exorcise evil spirits in the name of Jesus as Paul was doing at Ephesus (Acts 19:11-16).

Only when we reach the epistles does this method of teaching come into its own. It has already been shown how the New Testament writers, guided by the Spirit of God, adopted and adapted the literary structures of the time. This important current element of teaching, which would have carried great weight with the original readers, was used as a teaching method by all the epistle writers—Paul, James, Peter, John, Jude, and the anonymous author of Hebrews. Their Spirit-inspired teaching is in sharp contrast to the earlier attempt of the apostles James and John to apply to the Savior's ministry the previously mentioned example of Elijah calling fire to fall from Heaven upon his enemies (2 Kings 1:9-15); all they proved by this clumsy misapplication was that at the time they possessed plenty of zeal against Christ's opponents but little understanding that His mission involved saving lives, not destroying them (Luke 9:54-56).

The content, topics, and objects of the examples used in the epistles to disciple believers are strikingly unique and worthy of our consideration. Roman writers had anticipated a golden Augustan age based on the moral lessons of the past; but they were looking for a human solution to the evils of the time and were, therefore, looking in the wrong direction. Examples in the epistles of the New Testament have an added spiritual dimension. We would, perhaps, be justified in Christianizing the statement of the historian Livy and say, "One thing which makes the study of Scripture beneficial and fruitful is this, that you behold the lessons of every kind of example as upon a famous monument; from these you may choose for yourself and for your church what to imitate, and mark for avoidance what is shameful in its conception and shameful in its result."[7]

But we do not have to go outside the Bible and borrow statements from elsewhere. The apostle John made the point in the clearest form possible when he wrote, "Beloved, do not imitate what is evil, but what is good" (3 John 11). A study of this kind is not intended to produce an exhaustive picture of the Christian life but to draw out some of the major principles involved. The following chapters trace the development of the concept of imitation, starting with repentance (involving the

---

7   Titus Livius, "Preface," *Ab urbe condita*, in Stephen Usher, *The Historians of Greece and Rome* (London, Methuen & Co, 1970), 167.

avoidance of bad examples), proceeding to examples of faith, and concluding with the imitation and setting of good examples of Christ-like Christian living.

Chapter 3
AVOIDING BAD EXAMPLES

"**D**O NOT IMITATE WHAT IS evil" (3 John 11). How some Christians hate anything negative! While being negative for the sake of it is an unhealthy attitude to adopt, the Bible presents us with a healthy balance of the negative and the positive. The Ten Commandments themselves are in their basic form 80 percent negative but, when summarized or combined, add up to the glorious positives of loving God and our neighbors (Matt. 22:36-40; Rom. 13:9-10). Sometimes, being negative can be the most positive step you can take!

John's third epistle was written to Gaius, a godly man who was experiencing a very nasty case of exclusivism, controlling, and bullying in the form of a church leader by the name of Diotrephes. These two men could hardly have been more different. Gaius put others first; Diotrephes put himself first. Gaius was a loving servant, Diotrephes a malicious tyrant; Gaius promoted fellowship by welcoming visiting

Christians; Diotrephes created schism by driving them away and excommunicating those who did welcome them (3 John 5-10). There was, perhaps, a danger of Gaius being overawed and wrongly influenced by the behavior of Diotrephes, hence John's diagnosis of the spiritual condition of Diotrephes—"He who does evil has not seen God"—and his timely advice to Gaius— "Beloved, do not imitate what is evil" (3 John 11).

The right and proper starting point in an examination of the doctrine of imitation must be a consideration of those exposed by God as bad examples to be avoided. For the most part, negative examples of bad behavior to be avoided are drawn from the Old Testament, a fact which certainly contradicts those who have little or no time for the Old Testament. In the words of the Puritan John Owen (1616-1683), "Old Testament examples are New Testament instructions."[8]

The second epistle of Peter and the epistle of Jude are full of negative teaching due to the danger of believers being led astray by false teachers and their followers (2 Peter 2:1-2; Jude 4). A terrible picture is drawn of the wrong examples being followed and where following such examples leads. We need to pay heed to such warnings in these days, when there are multitudes of false teachers. To make matters even worse, undiscerning believers tend to oppose those who, in the course of contending for the faith (Jude 3), dare to expose false teachers and their

---

8   Isaac Thomas, *A Puritan Golden Treasury* (Edinburgh: Banner of Truth, 1977), 96.

false doctrines. The infiltration of false teachers into the church may happen in secret (2 Peter 2:1; Jude 4), but any who can see it happening are surely committing a sin of omission if they ignore it or sweep it under the carpet.

Without much comment, Jude names the individual Old Testament characters on which these false teachers are modelled. "Woe to them! For they have gone in the way of Cain, have run greedily in the error of Balaam for profit, and perished in the rebellion of Korah" (Jude 11). Cain murdered his righteous brother (1 John 3:12), and false teachers are no less than the spiritual murderers of those they lead astray. Balaam fell for the love of money (2 Peter 2:15), which proved to be a "root of all evil" both for him and for the Israelites he led into idolatry and immorality (Num. 31:8, 16; Rev. 2:14). How often have false teachers been exposed in connection with covetousness or immorality! Korah and his followers were not satisfied with their Levitical role as God's servants but took too much upon themselves by aspiring to the priesthood (Num. 16:7-9). The thirst of false teachers for positions of authority and power sometimes amounts to sheer blasphemy.

However, both Peter and Jude look not at individuals but at groups as their main examples of the eternal punishment reserved for the ungodly (2 Peter 2:4-6; Jude 5-7). Their warnings, like those issued concerning false teachers, are timely reminders for the church in these days when the doctrine of eternal punishment is attacked and ridiculed by "churchmen" among others. For their earliest examples to be avoided, Peter and Jude take us right back to the early chapters of the Old Testament and to the similarly maligned book of Genesis.

WARNINGS FROM GENESIS

Peter, giving "an example to those who afterward would live ungodly" (2 Peter 2:6), lists three groups from Genesis: "the angels who sinned" (2:4), "the world of the ungodly" in the time of the flood (2:5), and "the cities of Sodom and Gomorrah" (2:6). In Jude's parallel passage, the first and last of these appear, the latter "set forth as an example, suffering the vengeance of eternal fire" (Jude 6-7).

Looking at these chronologically, one can easily detect the same types of wickedness exemplified by the false teachers. According to Jude, the sin of the angels was that they "did not keep their proper domain, but left their own abode" (Jude 6), exactly the same kind of rebellious dissatisfaction, albeit on a larger scale, as that later displayed by Korah and his followers. The penalty for such transgression was that God "cast them down to hell and delivered them into chains of darkness, to be reserved for judgment" (2 Peter 2:4). He has reserved them "in everlasting chains under darkness for the judgment of the great day" (Jude 6).

Jesus specifically described Hell as "the everlasting fire prepared for the devil and his angels" (Matt. 25:41), but He warned people of the danger of going there. Peter and Jude have a similar message for an ungodly world. The flood washed away an entire ungodly generation apart from Noah and his seven relatives (2 Peter 2:5). But in Peter's day, those who would demythologize Scripture were already at work. This example of punishment was ignored by those who wanted to ridicule the whole idea of the Second Coming of Christ and the Day of Judgment (2 Pet. 3:3-7). The attempt to demythologize parts of the Bible—and the book of Genesis, in particular—is still a convenient way of attempting to undermine the truths about the judgment to come.

The destruction of Sodom and Gomorrah is also treated as a warning example of sinners "suffering the vengeance of eternal fire" (Jude 7). Sexual immorality—and, on this occasion, homosexuality in particular—brought upon its perpetrators the judgment of God. Peter describes the sins of Sodom and Gomorrah as "filthy conduct" and "lawless deeds" (2 Peter 2:7-8). Those who would scoff at such warnings in these so-called enlightened days should also bear in mind the words of the Lord Jesus Christ. He warned that the enlightened, who ought to know better than the people of Sodom and Gomorrah but who still reject His ways, will face an even worse judgment than that suffered by Sodom and Gomorrah (Matt. 10:15; 11:24). The importance of all these examples was well underlined by Albert Barnes: "They were a demonstration that God disapproved of the crimes for which they were punished, and would disapprove of the same crimes in every age and in every land. The punishment of one wicked man or people always becomes a warning to all others."[9]

However, this is not the whole story. Peter balances this terrible picture of God's power to punish the ungodly by referring also to Noah and Lot, men who were far from perfect but righteous through their faith in God and who stood out against the wickedness which surrounded them. In numerical terms, their respective influence was minimal; those saved along with them did not even reach double figures. But they were precious in God's eyes and were rescued from judgment. Such deliverance of the godly is properly appreciated and valued only when it is balanced by a solemn understanding that God will just as surely punish the ungodly (2 Peter 2:9).

Jude provides an even more alarming example, based on the books of Exodus and Numbers: "the Lord, having saved the people out of the land of Egypt, afterward destroyed those who did not believe" (Jude 5). To have God's enemies at that time, such as Pharaoh (Rom. 9:17) and his magicians (2 Tim. 3:8-9) exposed as bad examples is no great surprise; but here we find God's own chosen people, Israel, portrayed as such. It is bound to come as a shock when even the "goodies" turn out to be "baddies"; but having inherited a sinful nature from Adam, all have sinned (Rom. 5:12, 14), hence our need to beware of copying bad examples,

---

9   Alfred Barnes, *A Popular Family Commentary on the New Testament*, Vol. 10 (London, The Gresham Publishing Company, 1868), 241.

especially when by the people of God. This theme is developed in Hebrews and 1 Corinthians.

WARNINGS FROM THE WANDERINGS OF THE CHILDREN OF ISRAEL

"Today, if you will hear His voice, do not harden your hearts as in the rebellion, in the day of trial in the wilderness, where your fathers tested Me, tried Me, and saw My works forty years, Therefore I was angry with that generation, and said, 'They always go astray in their heart, and they have not known my ways.' So I swore in My wrath, 'They shall not enter My rest'" (Heb. 3:7-11).

The third and fourth chapters of the epistle to the Hebrews are largely in the form of a commentary upon this quotation of Psalm 95:7-11. In the context, these warnings were directed toward Jews who had professed faith in Christ but who were now having second thoughts due to persecution and the like; they were consequently in danger of abandoning Christ to return to a Christless Judaism. What they were contemplating was highly blasphemous: the putting of Christ "to an open shame" (Heb. 6:6). In other words, they were about to make a public example of the Person and work of Christ Himself as evil things to be avoided. On one occasion during Christ's lifetime, many of His disciples had taken such a backward step due to their inability to cope with His teaching; the twelve apostles had nobly refused to copy this bad example, though even one of them later turned out to be a traitor (John 6:66-71).

These are not theoretical or hypothetical cases. There is a wide application to anybody who has professed faith in Christ but who is toying with the thought of leaving Christ and returning to a Christless way of life. The lesson is basic, and the readers of the epistle to the Hebrews were stuck at the first stage of needing to learn from the bad examples of the past; they were still spiritual babies (Heb. 5:11-14).

The behavior of the children of Israel is a solemn warning against starting without finishing. They had made a positive beginning by leaving their old way of life—slavery in Egypt— under the leadership of Moses; but the next forty years saw them continually provoking God to anger with the result that they fell dead in the wilderness because of their sins (Heb. 3:16-17). Their combined disobedience and lack of faith prevented them reaching the Promised Land and the promised rest. Today, God holds before His people the prospect of a better promised land—a heavenly city (Heb. 13:14)—and a better promised rest, a heavenly rest (Rev. 14:13). The first main division of Hebrews ends with the obvious application of the example set by the children of Israel: "Let us therefore be diligent to enter that rest, lest anyone fall according to the same example of disobedience" (Heb. 4:11). Our neglect or rejection of the one and only way of salvation is an offense against God just as punishable as their disobedience to His law (Heb. 2:1-3). Comparable was the earlier infidelity of

Esau, as one who had been only too ready to sacrifice long-term spiritual blessings for short-term physical gains (Heb. 12:16-17). Such disobedience and unbelief are major examples to avoid.

The experiences of the children of Israel are also cited as examples in a local church situation, where they were painfully relevant. Paul's first epistle to the Corinthians reveals a church in great disarray, similarly stuck at the stage of spiritual babyhood and weighed down with ungodliness (1 Cor. 3:1-3). Like the readers of Hebrews, but in a somewhat different sense, they were still at the first stage of needing to learn about the avoidance of ungodliness. To instruct them, Paul drew numerous examples from the behavior of the children of Israel (1 Cor. 10:1-11). They had enjoyed the Old Testament equivalents of baptism and the Lord's Supper (vv. 1-4), but the possession of these privileges did not prevent the vast majority of them falling dead in the wilderness and failing to reach the Promised Land (v. 5).

"Now these things became our examples, to the intent that we should not lust after evil things as they also lusted" (1 Cor. 10:6). Some commentators treat the "lusting" mentioned here as a general description of the various "works of the flesh" displayed by the children of Israel and listed in the next few verses. The Corinthian church was full of evil things, well exemplified by the children of Israel. Others see here a specific reference to the example set in Numbers 11:4-5, where the children of Israel and their fellow travelers developed a craving for meat and, with relevance to the warnings just considered in the epistle to the Hebrews, looked longingly backward to Egypt and to the wonderful diet they claimed to have once enjoyed there. The abandonment of the journey and a return to Egypt was always in their minds (Num. 14:2-4). Whichever interpretation of this verse is correct, the principle is clear. Charles Hodge comments, "The Israelites and the facts of their history were our types, because we shall be conformed to them if we do not exercise caution. Our doom will correspond to theirs. They therefore stand as warnings to us."[10]

"And do not become idolaters as were some of them. As it is written, 'The people sat down to eat and drink, and rose up to play'" (1 Cor. 10:7, quoting Exod. 32:6). While Moses was on Mount Sinai receiving the Ten Commandments and the details of the law and the Tabernacle, it was no time at all before the people fell into idolatry and its associated abominations. About three thousand men died as a result (Exod. 32:28). In the preceding chapters, Paul had dealt with the problem of idolatry in Corinth and the question the church had asked him concerning food offered to idols (1 Cor. 8:1). Some boasted of their knowledge that idols were non-existent (v. 4) and had no concern about being seen eating in an idol's temple (v. 10); but this was causing problems to those who had been converted from a belief in idols (v. 7) and was therefore not a wise and loving act. Besides, on returning to this subject in the latter half of chapter ten, Paul

---

10   Charles Hodge, *A Commentary on the First Epistle to the Corinthians* (London, Banner of Truth reprint, 1958), 176.

pointed out that toying with "non-existent" idols is not as innocent as it may appear at first sight: behind the worship of non-existent idols is the worship of actual demons (1 Cor. 10:19-20). The idolatrous example of the children of Israel was of great relevance to the Corinthians: "Therefore, my beloved, flee from idolatry" (10:14). Idolatry is something which should be left behind in the Christian's former unconverted life (1 Cor. 12:2).

"Nor let us commit sexual immorality, as some of them did, and in one day twenty-three thousand fell" (1 Cor. 10:8, with reference to Num. 25). We have already considered Peter's and Jude's warnings against immorality based on Old Testament examples. Here, taking the children of Israel as his example, Paul adds his voice on the same subject. The Corinthians needed the warning, since they were tolerating a case of immorality within the church, which even pagans would not permit (1 Cor. 5:1). Paul had previously told them to avoid company with the sexually immoral and now had to underline that point by stating that his instruction specifically referred to sexually immoral people who claimed to be Christians (1 Cor. 5:9-11). His straight command to the believer is, "Flee sexual immorality" (1 Cor. 6:18).

"Nor let us tempt Christ, as some of them also tempted, and were destroyed by serpents" (1 Cor. 10:9, with reference to Num. 21:5-6). Testing and tempting God may not sound quite as serious as acts of idolatry and immorality; but in the case in question, many of the children of Israel died as a result. That the Corinthians were also in danger of committing the same sin can be gleaned from

Paul's questions: "Or do we provoke the Lord to jealousy? Are we stronger than He?" (1 Cor. 10:22).

"Nor complain, as some of them also complained, and were destroyed by the destroyer" (1 Cor. 10:10, with particular reference to Num. 16:11, 41, and 49). Again, when compared with the more scandalous sins, complaining, grumbling, and murmuring may sound trivial; but these were, in fact, the most repeated sins committed by the children of Israel. On the occasion recorded in Numbers 16, at least 14,700 died. The Corinthians also were guilty of this repeated sin. Paul had to plead with them to repent of their divisions, contentions, envy, and strife (1 Cor. 1:10-11; 3:3; 11:18). There are clear indications in 2 Corinthians that some were murmuring against the apostle Paul himself and questioning his authority in exactly the same way as Korah and others spoke against Moses in the wilderness. One of the apostle John's condemnations of Diotrephes, with whom we began this chapter, was that he was "prating against us with malicious words" (3 John 10). In God's eyes, evil words, as well as evil acts, count as sin.

It is shocking to realize that it is possible for all these things to go on among the people of God. To the Corinthians, Paul could have well used the phrase, "If the shoe fits, wear it." Among his comments on Hebrews 4:11 concerning the example of the children of Israel, John Owen said, "It is better to have an example than to be made an example of divine displeasure."[11]

---

11   John Owen, *Exposition of the Epistle to the Hebrews: An Abridgement by M. J. Tryon* (London: E. Wilmhurst, n.d.), 72.

However, the Corinthians were committing the very same sins as the children of Israel, and the repeated references to Israelite deaths in the verses considered above were also painfully relevant to them. Their lamentable imitation of the Lord's Supper (1 Cor. 11:20-21) "in an unworthy manner" (v. 27) was itself resulting in fresh up-to-date examples of many being struck down with illness and death (v. 30).

Paul closes his list of Israelite examples with these words: "Now all these things happened to them as examples, and they were written for our admonition, upon whom the ends of the ages have come. Therefore let him who thinks he stands take heed lest he fall" (1 Cor. 10:11-12). If we criticize the Corinthian church for getting stuck at the point of needing to exercise repentance by learning the avoidance of sin from bad examples, we must nevertheless not underestimate this stage, which should play an important part in the spiritual development of every believer. Babyhood should not be despised; but it should only be a passing phase, and we should grow out of it, as taught by Peter. "Therefore, laying aside all malice, all deceit, hypocrisy, envy, and all evil speaking, as newborn babes, desire the pure milk of the word, that you may grow thereby" (1 Peter 2:1-2). Paul had already written to the Corinthians: "Do you not know that the unrighteous will not inherit the kingdom of God? Do not be deceived. Neither fornicators, nor idolaters, nor adulterers, nor homosexuals, nor sodomites, nor thieves, nor covetous, nor drunkards, nor revilers, nor extortioners will inherit the kingdom of God" (1 Cor. 6:9-10).

These things belonged to their past lives before Christ saved them (v. 11); it would be hypocritical of them to continue in fellowship with anybody professing to be a Christian "who is sexually immoral, or covetous, or an idolater, or a reviler, or a drunkard, or an extortioner" (1 Cor. 5:11).

But even when he wrote again to the Corinthians, Paul still had his doubts and suspected that many of them had not yet managed to learn the lesson of avoiding bad examples (2 Cor. 12:20-21). There was a terrible danger of them remaining stuck at this preliminary stage, and Paul had so wanted to lead them forward to the next stage, hence his positive instructions, "Therefore I urge you, imitate me" (1 Cor. 4:16) and "Imitate me, just as I also imitate Christ" (1 Cor. 11:1). We also need to advance in that direction.

The negative is very important, but it needs to be balanced by the positive. This was a significant feature of Paul's teaching on the Christian life because there are two sides to it. "Put on the Lord Jesus Christ, and make no provision for the flesh, to fulfill its lusts" (Rom. 13:14); "Walk in the Spirit, and you shall not fulfill the lust of the flesh" (Gal. 5:16). Of even greater relevance to our subject is the full statement of John, the first half of which began this chapter, "Beloved, do not imitate what is evil, but what is good" (3 John 11). We are unlikely to follow good examples unless we avoid bad examples; conversely, we are unlikely to avoid bad examples unless we copy good examples. While bad examples warn us against sins of commission, we also need good examples to guide us away from sins of omission. In fact, teaching by means of examples in the New Testament is even more of a positive exercise than a negative one. Whereas negative examples have been considered in one chapter, there is enough material concerning positive examples to warrant three chapters. John Owen, commenting on Hebrews 6:12, wrote, "The providing of examples for us in the Scriptures, which we ought to imitate and follow, is an effectual way of teaching, and a great fruit of the care and kindness of God toward us."[12]

---

12 Owen, 104.

Chapter 4
COPYING GOOD EXAMPLES:
THE IMITATION OF FAITH

"**B**ELOVED, DO NOT IMITATE WHAT is evil, but what is good. He who does good is of God" (3 John 11). Having dealt scathingly with Diotrephes, an example of an evildoer who apparently hadn't even seen God, John encouraged Gaius to continue on the good path he was already treading. He was able to point Gaius to another man of God like him, a doer of good and a follower of the truth, who was worthy of his continued imitation: "Demetrius has a good testimony from all, and from the truth itself" (3 John 12).

The imitation of good examples is a large topic in the New Testament epistles. A good starting point would be where the Corinthians, considered in the previous chapter, had to begin. Many of them needed to exercise repentance and to apply the avoidance of bad examples; they also needed to submit themselves to self-examination particularly with regard to their faith. Paul emphasized this toward the end of 2 Corinthians: "Examine yourselves as to whether you are in the faith. Test yourselves" (2 Cor. 13:5). For many of them, this may have led to a realization that they were still unconverted and to a true conversion experience. Repentance and saving faith are the true starting points of the Christian life.

THE EMPHASIS PLACED UPON EXAMPLES OF FAITH

The subject of faith occupies a unique position in the New Testament's approach to teaching by examples. In this may be observed a sharp contrast with the approach taken by the moralizing historians who were active in New Testament times. Their histories reveal clearly the kinds of examples, good and bad, which they wished to impress upon their readers. A brief consideration of three of these historians will highlight the uniqueness of the New Testament.

The most thorough exponent of this method of teaching was Livy in his history of Rome. In addition to some constitutional subjects, he specifically and repeatedly labeled as examples actions involving the following moral topics: discord and harmony, morals of men at home and on military service, warding off crimes, military discipline, treachery, the outcome of revolt, cruelty, public loyalty, humanity and clemency, mastery and servitude, changes of fortune, avoiding similar disasters, greed, examples which rebound on their originators, moderation.[13] The main topics labeled as examples by Josephus (born AD 37/8) in his Jewish Antiquities (a kind of free paraphrase of the Old Testament) were virtue, kindness, and reverence.[14] Tacitus, in his histories of imperial Rome, regularly emphasized examples of virtue, constancy, faithfulness, death, punishment, and clemency and, like Josephus, often related examples to religious topics.[15]

For the writers of the New Testament epistles, however, there was only one topic which they repeatedly highlighted for the purpose of giving examples. Notably, it was not a matter of morals or behavior but faith, a spiritual subject. This must have been very striking to the original readers of the epistles. With the benefit of hindsight, we should not be so surprised; the 260 chapters of the New Testament contain no less than 244 occurrences of the noun "faith" and 246 of the verb "believe." It was the most obvious topic for underlining by means of examples. In prefacing his work with his reasons for writing it, an ancient historian would naturally give away some of the subjects he intended to highlight in it; the preface to Livy's history contains many moral terms, which often appear, sometimes in great numbers, when he highlights specific examples of behavior to imitate or avoid. The New Testament

---

13   Throughout the thirty-five books remaining from the original 142 in Titus Livius, *The Complete Livy: The History of Rome "Ab Urbe Condita,"* www.bybliotech.org, 2012, Kindle edition.

14   Flavius Josephus, *Antiquitates Judaicae* in *The Works of Flavius Josephus,* translated by William Whiston (James S. Virtue: London, n.d.) 29-603.

15   Cornelius Tacitus, *Annals and Histories: Tacitus* (London: Everyman, 2009).

writers do exactly the same when giving the reasons for the writing of Scripture; and when doing so, the subject to which they repeatedly draw our attention is that of faith:

- "These are written that you may *believe* that Jesus is the Christ, the Son of God, and that *believing* you may have life in His name" (John 20:31, emphasis mine).
- "For I am not ashamed of the gospel of Christ, for it is the power of God to salvation for everyone who believes . . . For in it the righteousness of God is revealed from *faith to faith*; as it is written, 'The just shall live by *faith*'" (Rom. 1:16-17, emphasis mine).
- "From childhood you have known the Holy Scriptures, which are able to make you wise for salvation through *faith* which is in Christ Jesus" (2 Tim. 3:15, emphasis mine).
- "These things I have written to you who *believe* in the name of the Son of God, that you may know that you have eternal life, and that you may continue to *believe* in the name of the Son of God" (1 John 5:13, emphasis mine).

Paul's description of faith in Christ as being the means of access to the righteousness of God "from first to last" (Rom. 1:17, NIV) finds ample expression in the New Testament's emphasis on the imitation of faith.

THE EXAMPLE OF SAVING FAITH

Nine times out of ten, the imitation of Christians as a route to salvation consists of the dangerous error of salvation by works because the usual object of such imitation tends to be the Christian lifestyle. This should not be confused with the imitation of the step of saving faith in Christ taken by others in becoming Christians. As seen earlier, Christ condemned Jewish leaders for witnessing but failing to imitate the step of saving faith taken by those they labeled "sinners" (Matt. 21:31-32). Such imitation is entirely biblical and to be commended.

The apostle Paul could point to his own experience. As an unbelieving sinner, saved by the grace of God in Christ, he was an outstanding example of Christ's perfect patience and readiness to accept all who would exercise the same step of saving faith in the future. "This is a faithful saying and worthy of all acceptance, that Christ Jesus came into the world to save sinners, of whom I am chief. However, for this reason I obtained mercy, that in me first Jesus Christ might show all longsuffering, as a pattern to those who are going to believe in Him for everlasting life" (1 Tim. 1:15-16).

Just as in the previous chapter we saw examples of the disobedience of unbelief leading to God's judgment (Heb. 4:2, 11), so at the beginning and end of his epistle to the Romans, Paul stresses the obedience of faith in Christ as his goal and as the essential route to salvation (Rom. 1:5; 16:26). In the middle of the same epistle, a whole chapter (Rom. 4) is devoted to the greatest example of faith in the Old Testament, Abraham (see also Gal. 3:6-9). Quoting the Scriptural fact that before he was circumcised, "Abraham believed God, and it was accounted to him for righteousness" (Rom. 4:3), Paul emphasizes that "it was not written for his sake alone that it was imputed to him, but also for us. It shall be imputed to us who believe in Him who raised up Jesus our Lord from the dead" (Rom. 4:23-24). Abraham is "the father of all those who believe, though they are uncircumcised" and of all the circumcised "who also walk in the steps of the faith which our father Abraham had while still uncircumcised" (Romans 4:11-12). His faith in the living God is therefore an example equally applicable to Jews and Gentiles.

Later, Paul goes on to express his thanksgiving to God that his readers had taken the vital step of obedience to the example of the teaching they had received. "But God be thanked that though you were slaves of sin, yet you obeyed from the heart that form [literally "type/pattern/model"] of doctrine to which you were delivered. And having been set free from sin, you became slaves of righteousness" (Rom. 6:17-18). In other words, they had been converted as the result of following the example of obeying the gospel by repenting of their sin and trusting in Christ.

The great importance of Romans 6:17 was stressed by Dr. Martyn Lloyd-Jones (1899-1981) as follows: "I venture to say that it is one of the most important and pivotal verses. That is so because it contains one of the clearest definitions found in the

New Testament as to what exactly it means to be a Christian."[16] His summary is valuable:

> I sum up the Apostle's teaching about 'the form of doctrine' in this way. The essence of sin is disobedience of God, His Word and His way; and therefore the essence of the opposite, which is faith, is obedience to God. The Christian man is a man who obeys God. How? He obeys God's Word, he obeys God's Gospel, he obeys everything that God has said. That is why in the first chapter in the fifth verse the Apostle talks about "the obedience of faith."[17]

As will be shown in a later chapter, faith was also one of the examples which Paul urged Timothy, as a young pastor, to set for others. True saving faith is not theoretical but outwardly practical. This can best be seen in the epistle to the Hebrews, the writer of which was the most thorough New Testament exponent of teaching by means of examples of faith.

EXAMPLES OF LIVING BY FAITH

Having warned his readers about the dangerous consequences of following a bad example by abandoning their faith in

---

16   D. Martyn Lloyd-Jones, *Romans: An Exposition of Chapter 6: The New Man* (London: Banner of Truth, 1972), 205.

17   Ibid, 219.

Christ (Heb. 4:1-11), the writer seeks to take them forward (6:1). Proceeding to the next stage, he encourages them to "imitate those who through faith and patience inherit the promises" (6:12). Abraham is briefly introduced as an example: "And so, after he had patiently endured, he obtained the promise" (6:15). However, the exhortation does not receive its full outworking until chapter eleven, which is prefaced by a reminder of the need for patience and faith: "For you have need of endurance, so that after you have done the will of God, you may receive the promise: . . . 'Now the just shall live by faith; but if anyone draws back, my soul has no pleasure in him'" (10:36, 38).

To anybody familiar with Roman literature, Hebrews 11 would have appeared similar to a single chapter extracted from a work like that of Valerius Maximus, where examples of various kinds of behavior had been collected and listed together under specific topics as described in chapter two. There would, of course, be major differences: the characters are Jewish; the context is the Old Testament and the topic is faith in the living God.

Commentaries on Hebrews 11 are numerous, and so a summary will suffice here. The writer commences with our own faith in God's work of creation. Then the examples of faith begin from the book of Genesis with Abel's acceptable sacrifice; Enoch's walking with God and pleasing Him; Noah's heeding of God's warning about the flood; Abraham's exodus from his homeland to live in the land of promise; Sarah's conception; Abraham's willingness to sacrifice his one and only hope in the belief that God could raise the dead; Isaac's blessing upon his sons; Jacob's blessing upon Joseph's sons, prophesying that the younger would be greater; and Joseph's prophecy of the Exodus.

As was shown earlier, the story of the Exodus was marred by some terrible examples of unbelief. But there were also some great examples of faith. The writer continues by concentrating on Moses: hidden through the faith of his parents, choosing to suffer with God's people rather than enjoying the pleasures of sin, leaving Egypt, fearing God rather than man, and keeping the Passover. When the children of Israel reached the Red Sea, they trusted God and crossed successfully. The Egyptians tried to cross and failed. The children of Israel saw the walls of Jericho tumble down, and Rahab survived through becoming a traitor to God's enemies and trusting herself to His care among His people. At that point, the list of examples in Hebrews 11 breaks down through sheer weight of numbers, turning instead into a summary of names and of things achieved or suffered by those who trusted God.

These were the very people concerning whom the writer had said, "Imitate those who through faith and patience inherit the promises" (6:12). Though they had not actually received these promises in their lifetime, they had seen them from a distance and were assured of receiving them in the future (11:13, 39). As the fulfilment of their faith, they awaited the coming of "something better" (11:40), namely the Lord Jesus Christ Himself. The Savior Himself testified that Abraham, for one, looked forward to His coming and rejoiced (John 8:56). But Abraham was not the only one. To His followers, Jesus was able to say, "But blessed are your eyes for they see, and your ears for they hear; for assuredly, I say to you that many prophets and righteous men desired to see what you see, and did not see it, and to hear what you hear, and did not hear it" (Matt. 13:16-17).

As far as the first coming of Christ was concerned, New Testament believers had this advantage over Old Testament believers. However, as far as His second coming and the eternal kingdom are concerned, we find ourselves in exactly the same position as Old Testament believers and in need of the same kind of trust in God. Abraham "waited for the city which has foundations, whose builder and maker is God" (11:10). The Old Testament believers "desire a better, that is, a heavenly country. Therefore God is not ashamed to be called their God, for He has prepared a city for them" (11:16). Though living after the first coming of Christ, we are no different in this respect. "For here we have no continuing city, but we seek the one to come" (13:14). For that reason the faith and patience displayed by the Old Testament heroes and heroines of faith is still worthy of our imitation.

One obvious feature of the Hebrews 11 list of examples of faith is that faith is never seen there in isolation. The faith to be imitated is never a lifeless and fruitless so-called faith. As described by Paul, it must always be a case of "faith working through love" (Gal. 5:6). Nearly forty different outworkings of faith are described in Hebrews 11. It is in this light that we should view James' much shorter passage of examples illustrating the workings of faith (James 2:20-25). To suggest that James teaches salvation by works is to misunderstand him completely. His subject is still faith but a living faith that makes a difference to life. In the epistle of James, we meet the selfsame examples of what Abraham and Rahab actually did as the outworking of their faith. Concerning Abraham, James asks, "Do you see that faith was working together with his works, and by works faith was made perfect?" (James 2:22)

Hebrews 11 is not quite the writer's last word on examples of faith. His long list of Old Testament examples could perhaps appear distant and as far removed from the days of the Roman Empire as New Testament times are from us today, though the experiences and sufferings described would have been painfully relevant to the first readers. But there were more recent examples to imitate, and the writer signs off on this subject with a reference to them: "Remember those who rule over you, who have spoken the word of God to you, whose faith follow, considering the outcome of their conduct" (Heb. 13:7).

In the context, this may well refer to their deceased leaders; the best way of honoring their memory is to be faithful to their faith and example. John Owen has the following helpful comment on this verse:

> To follow their faith is to "imitate" it; and this may
> be viewed objectively, for the faith which they
> taught, believed and professed; also subjectively, for
> the grace of faith in them whereby they believed the
> truth; and it is in this latter sense the word is to be
> specially understood here. It was that faith whereby
> they glorified God in all that they did and suffered
> for the name of Jesus Christ.[18]

This verse can be applied as an exhortation to imitate the
faith not simply of believers we have only read about but also of
those with whom we have been personally acquainted. The next
chapter will go on to consider other aspects of Christian living,
for which we can find our examples both in the Scriptures and
in our own experience of fellowship with other believers. The
apostle Paul, personally known to the readers of his letters but
known to us only in the pages of Scripture, could say both to
them and to us, "Imitate me" (1 Cor. 4:16; 11:1). His plea to the
Galatians was, "Brethren, I urge you to become like me" (Gal.
4:12). Whereas, Paul had turned from legalism to faith in Christ,
they were now doing the very opposite by wrongly thinking
that adherence to the Jewish law was essential to their salvation.
To the Philippians, he wrote, "Brethren, join in following my
example, and note those who so walk, as you have us for a pattern"
(Phil. 3:17). We know for a fact that the Thessalonians took this

---

18   Owen, 272.

kind of instruction seriously. With thanks to God, Paul could write to them, "You became followers [literally "imitators"] of us" (1 Thess. 1:6).

When in Christ, do as godly Christians do!

Chapter 5
COPYING GOOD EXAMPLES: THE IMITATION OF GODLINESS

"YOU BECAME FOLLOWERS OF US," Paul could say to the Thessalonians (1 Thess. 1:6). Unlike the Corinthians, they had eagerly turned away from bad examples, such as idolatry (v. 9) and had already advanced to a positive and profitable form of imitation. While faith itself is the most repeated single topic commended for imitation in the New Testament epistles, it is far from being the only one. In addition to imitating faithful believers in their *trust*, we are also encouraged to imitate them in their *teaching*, in their *toils*, and in their *trials*.

The apostle Paul, having been responsible for the founding of so many of the churches to which he wrote, found himself in the highly privileged but responsible position of being an example to be set before them for their imitation. Yet, as we shall see later, this fact was not a symptom of big-headedness or of power-madness but was tempered and balanced by a most important condition: "Imitate me, just as I also imitate Christ" (1 Cor. 11:1).

THE TEACHING OF THE GODLY

Ungodly behavior so often goes hand in hand with false doctrine; as we have already seen, Peter and Jude had plenty of warnings to give concerning this. The Corinthian church also was in danger of going astray not only in practice but also in doctrine. Paul found it necessary to remind them of his fatherly role in the founding of the church in Corinth. For eighteen months, he had taught them God's Word (Acts 18:11); but since then, they had not advanced from spiritual babyhood (1 Cor. 3:1-2). It was high time for a refresher course, and so he had sent Timothy to them. "In Christ Jesus I have begotten you through the gospel. Therefore I urge you, imitate me. For this reason I have sent Timothy to you, who is my beloved and faithful son in the Lord, who will remind you of my ways in Christ, as I teach everywhere in every church" (1 Cor. 4:15-17).

In later years, as Paul was approaching his execution, Timothy himself was to receive a timely reminder, when he could have been in danger of wavering. Hymenaeus and Philetus had swerved from the truth by means of false doctrine and were upsetting the faith of some (2 Tim. 2:17-18). Others were willing to listen to anybody and, though "always learning," were "never able to come to the knowledge of the truth" (2 Tim. 3:7). Yet others would have "itching ears" and would turn away from the truth to listen to anybody who would teach them just what they wanted to hear (2 Tim. 4:3-4).

Paul, therefore, in his last letter, encouraged Timothy to make every effort to be faithful to true sound doctrine. Among his words of encouragement, Paul pointed back to his own example: "Hold fast the pattern of sound words which you have heard from me, in faith and love which are in Christ Jesus. That good thing which was committed to you, keep by the Holy Spirit who dwells in us" (2 Tim. 1:13-14). In a sermon on verse thirteen entitled "The Form of Sound Words," C.H. Spurgeon (1834-1892) paraphrased the apostle's intentions as follows:

> Timothy, when I have preached to you, you have heard certain grand outlines of truth; you have heard from me the great system of faith in Jesus Christ; in my writings and public speakings you have heard me continually insist upon a certain pattern or form of faith; now I bid you, my dearly beloved son in the gospel, "Hold fast the form of sound words, which thou hast heard of me, in faith and love which is in Christ Jesus."[19]

In the same sermon, Spurgeon stressed that a form of sound words must be scriptural about God, about man, and about the

---

19 Charles H. Spurgeon, "The Form of Sound Words," *New Park Street Pulpit Vol. 2* no. 79 (London: Passmore & Alabaster, 1856), 201.

way of salvation. We may deduce that obedience to the example of good doctrine is essential not only to true conversion (as seen already from Romans 6:17) but also to continuation in the faith. These were timely reminders in those days, reminders which sadly are just as relevant in these days when we forget faithful teachers of the Word of God in favor of "every wind of doctrine" (Eph. 4:14) or more palatable teaching, which falls more pleasingly upon the ear. As ever, the example of the noble Bereans (Acts 17:11) is vital for us; we must check all teaching against the Scriptures. If we find it wanting, we should reject it; if we find it faithful to Scripture, we should receive and adhere to it, however unpleasant and unwelcome the truth may appear to be. Then we should teach it to others for them in turn to pass on (2 Tim. 2:2). In the example, it sets for our imitation the teaching of the godly is fundamental. But we must not allow it to stand in isolation.

THE TOILS OF THE GODLY

While sound doctrine is vital, there is a danger of stopping at this point and resting satisfied with a dead orthodoxy. Just as we must see faith as it is worked out in practice, so sound doctrine should be worked out in the life of the Christian. This is something which Paul had both taught and exemplified. The more doctrinal epistles, such as Romans and Ephesians, begin with long doctrinal sections but always reach a point where that doctrine has to be applied in practice. The key word "therefore" provides the link between doctrine and practice in both Romans 12:1 and Ephesians 4:1. Sound doctrine should lead to right practice, and right practice depends on sound doctrine.

Such had been Paul's approach to the Thessalonians. His teaching concerning the suddenness of Christ's second coming, and the future bodily resurrection of believers was intended to prevent them sleeping away their lives in deadly ignorance "as others do" (1 Thess. 5:6) and sorrowing for their dead "as others who have no hope" (1 Thess. 4:13). However, some of them, misled, perhaps, through their misunderstanding and misapplication of the doctrine of the second coming, had failed to make other right connections between doctrine and practice and were living in idleness rather than in accord with what Paul had taught them (2 Thess. 3:6). To correct them, he was able to point back not only to his teaching but also to the practical example he had set them himself: "For you yourselves know how you ought to follow us, for we were not disorderly among you; nor did we eat anyone's bread free of charge, but worked with labor and toil night and day, that we might not be a burden to any of you, not because we do not have authority, but to make ourselves an example of how you should follow us" (2 Thess. 3:7-9). The great weight Paul placed here upon setting a good example is well described by Matthew Poole (1624-1679). "What he required of others he practiced himself, and that in some cases for this end alone, that he might be an example; examples teaching more than precepts, especially in ministers."[20]

It comes as no surprise that in their own special way the Corinthians also needed a similar reminder of how to live the Christian life. In their case, it took the form of needing to learn how to be of benefit to others, rather than thinking of themselves and their own rights. Again, Paul could point to his personal example: "Give no offense, either to the Jews or to the Greeks or to the church of God, just as I also please all men in all things, not seeking my own profit, but the profit of many, that they may be saved. Imitate me, just as I also imitate Christ" (1 Cor. 10:32-11:1).

To the Philippians, Paul presented himself as one toiling in spiritual matters. Unlike some whose minds were set on earthly things (Phil. 3:19), he could speak of himself pressing on in spiritual progress, looking for the return of the Lord Jesus Christ (Phil. 3:14, 20). This is the mature way of thinking (v. 15), and the example is set forth for imitation: "Brethren, join in following my example, and note those who so walk, as you have us for a pattern" (v. 17). We can see that Paul was not egotistical about this in his reference here to others who were setting the same standard of example, without doubt including Timothy and Epaphroditus, both highly commended by Paul in Philippians 2:19-30 for their spirituality and tireless service.

---

20   Matthew Poole, *A Commentary on the Holy Bible Vol. 3* (London: Banner of Truth reprint, 1963), 769.

When we combine all these examples set by the apostle Paul, we get a more balanced picture of what a Christian should be—sound in doctrine but living out that doctrine in practice, heavenly minded but also of some earthly use. The Christian who is merely devotional and theoretical is out of order; so is the practicing Christian who has plenty of time for action but no time for doctrine. The third aspect that is linked to these in the experience of the apostle Paul is trials.

THE TRIALS OF THE GODLY

Timothy had been able to observe Paul, not only in his "doctrine, manner of life, purpose, faith," etc. (2 Tim. 3:10) but also in his trials, especially his persecutions and afflictions (v. 11). That this was not peculiar to Paul's experience is clear from his statement in verse twelve: "Yes, and all who desire to live godly in Christ Jesus will suffer persecution." We cannot possibly be faithful to Scripture if we fail to consider the trials of the godly.

The Thessalonians had become faithful imitators of the apostle Paul in this respect "having received the word in much affliction" (1 Thess. 1:6), which is portrayed to some extent in the historical account recorded in Acts 17:1-13. There, the initial hostility of the Jews toward the gospel is clear. How this opposition developed and continued is hinted at in 1 Thessalonians 2:14: "For you, brethren, became imitators of the churches of God which are in Judea in Christ Jesus. For you also suffered the same things from your own countrymen, just as they did from the Judeans." The object of imitation here was on a corporate rather than an individual level; churches can be good examples for other churches to imitate, though in this particular case, the imitation was not deliberate.

Persecution is not the only trial which can come to the Christian. The Epistle of James was addressed to some who were falling "into various trials" (1:2), including oppression by the rich (2:6), who were defrauding and taking advantage of those who were poor agricultural laborers (5:4-6). James repeatedly emphasized to these suffering brothers their great need of patience (1:3-4) and appropriately continued with an agricultural illustration, to which they would readily relate. "Therefore be patient, brethren, until the coming of the Lord. See how the farmer waits for the precious fruit of the earth, waiting patiently for it until it receives the early and latter rain. You also be patient" (5:7-8). James then backed up the lesson by means of Old Testament examples: "My brethren, take the prophets, who spoke in the name of the Lord, as an example of suffering and patience. Indeed we count them blessed who endure. You have heard of the perseverance of Job and seen the end intended by the Lord—that the Lord is very compassionate and merciful" (5:10-11).

Here, different forms of patience under suffering are exemplified. First comes that of the prophets, men like Jeremiah and Elijah, "a man with a nature like ours" (5:17), whom James cites as an example of fervent righteous praying and its effects (5:16-18). Such men were persecuted and opposed for the faithful proclamation of God's Word. While James refers to the blessedness of the prophets who endured persecution, Jesus had already pronounced a beatitude upon those who follow in their footsteps. "Blessed are you when they revile and persecute you, and say all kinds of evil against you falsely for My sake. Rejoice and be exceedingly glad, for great is your reward in heaven, for so they persecuted the prophets who were before you" (Matt. 5:11-12).

Second, James refers to the trials suffered by Job who, being under the direct attack of Satan, endured with great fortitude loss, bereavement, sickness, and false accusations by his friends, sufferings which would try the holiest of saints. James also mentions "the end intended by the Lord—that the Lord is very compassionate and merciful" (5:11) This reference to the final outcome of the example in question (seen also in Heb. 13:7) is very important in terms of the encouragement it would afford. Matthew Poole says of these examples in James, "As the example of their sufferings should prevent your discouragement, so the example of their patience should provoke your imitation, God having set them forth as examples of both, that if you suffer the same things, you may suffer with the same minds."[21]

However, the reactions and examples of godly men like Jeremiah, Elijah, and Job, though remarkable, were by no means

---

21   Matthew Poole, *Commentary on the Holy Bible Vol. 3* (London: Banner of Truth reprint, 1963), 896.

perfect. This is also true of the heroes of faith already considered in the previous chapter. There were times when the faith of men like Abraham, Moses, and the prophets appeared to waver and be on the level of the man who said to Jesus with tears in his eyes, "Lord, I believe; help my unbelief!" (Mark 9:24).

At this point, therefore, a further and higher dimension must be introduced, though its implications should be mind-blowing. Examples set by other Christians may be good, but they will never be perfect. For that reason, we feel that imitation of them is within our range. But Paul, in acknowledging the imperfections of his own example went a step further, going on to say, "Imitate me, just as I also imitate Christ" (1 Cor. 11:1). This is an important condition: another believer should be imitated only in so far as they are themselves imitating Christ. We may readily acknowledge the imitation of the perfect Christ as beyond us. C. H. Spurgeon, in his sermon "Portraits of Christ" based on Romans 8:29, expressed his amazement at the thought of being conformed to the image of Christ in these words:

> If I were to be like David I might hope it; if I were to be made like Josiah, or some of the ancient saints, I might think it possible; but to be like Christ, who is without spot or blemish, and the chief among ten thousand, and altogether lovely, I cannot hope it. I look, sir; I look, and look, and look again, till I turn away, tears filling my eyes, and I say, "Oh, it is

presumption for such a fallen worm as I, to hope to be like Christ."[22]

And yet Christians will not only see Christ and be like Him in glory but are also expected to be imitators of Him in the here and now! In fact, future likeness to Christ is a strong motive for present imitation of Him. "We know that when He is revealed, we shall be like Him, for we shall see Him as He is. And everyone who has this hope in Him purifies himself, just as He is pure" (1 John 3:2-3). That such sublime imitation is not only desirable but also possible is indicated by Paul's description of the Thessalonians: "You became followers [literally "imitators"] of us and of the Lord" (1 Thess. 1:6). If faith is the supreme topic to imitate, then Christ is the supreme Person to imitate. What an undertaking! In Him we have set before us not just "a man with a nature like ours" (James 5:17) but One "who is holy, harmless, undefiled, separate from sinners" (Heb. 7:26). Yet He became flesh and blood like us (Heb. 2:14, 17) and in so doing became our supreme example.

When in Christ, seek to do as Christ does!

---

22   Charles H. Spurgeon, "Portraits of Christ," *New Park Street Pulpit Vol. 7 no. 355* (London: Passmore & Alabaster, 1861), p. 64.

Chapter 6
COPYING GOOD EXAMPLES: THE IMITATION OF CHRIST

"**Y**OU BECAME FOLLOWERS OF US and of the Lord" (1 Thess. 1:6). In this and other passages, the imitation of Christ comes last but certainly not least. It is not an optional extra, but it is a subject which needs careful handling. If the imitation of other Christians can get twisted into a vain attempt at salvation by good works, how much more so the imitation of Christ Himself. The twin dangers inherent in a treatment of this subject were summarized by the Scottish theologian James Stalker (1848-1927) in the introduction to his book, *Imago Christi: The Example of Jesus Christ*:

> Whilst to Christian experience the imitation of Christ has always been inexpressibly precious, it has held, in evangelical preaching and literature, on the whole, only an equivocal position. The Moderatism

which in the last century nearly extinguished the religion of the country made much of the example of Christ. But it divorced it from His atonement, and urged men to follow Christ's example, without first making them acquainted with Him as the Saviour from sins that are past. The Evangelicals, in opposition to this, made Christ's atonement the burden of their testimony and, when His example was mentioned, were ever ready with, Yes, but His death is more important. Thus it happened that the two parties divided the truth between them, the example of Christ being the doctrine of the one and His atoning death that of the other.[23]

Although this sweeping statement may be a bit too clear-cut, it does underline the need for doctrine and practice to go hand in hand. Many have indeed made the fatal mistake of regarding the imitation of Christ as the way of salvation, though one cannot but marvel at their superficiality and underestimation of the impossible course upon which they have embarked. The famous Victorian novelist Charles Dickens (1812-1870) fell into this trap. He often mentioned the example of Christ in his letters to his children and in 1849 wrote a book especially for them entitled, *The Life of our Lord*, which is almost a paraphrase of the

---

23   James Stalker, *Imago Christi: the Example of Jesus Christ* (London: Hodder & Stoughton, 1889), 32.

Gospels. It was the last of his books to be published, appearing posthumously in 1934. Sadly and ominously, it ends on a very suspect note:

> Remember! It is Christianity to do good always even to those who do evil to us. It is Christianity to love our neighbour as ourself, and to do to all men as we would have them do to us. It is Christianity to be gentle, merciful, and forgiving, and to keep those qualities quiet in our own hearts, and never make a boast of them, or of our prayers or of our love of God, but always to show that we love Him by humbly trying to do right in everything. If we do this, and remember the life and lessons of Our Lord Jesus Christ, and try to act up to them, we may confidently hope that God will forgive us our sins and mistakes, and enable us to live and die in Peace.[24]

While much that is said here may be good, it still boils down to the vain hope of salvation by works; he said nothing about trusting in Christ's sacrifice on the cross for the forgiveness of our sins. According to Dickens, the early Christians "carried crosses as their sign, because upon a cross He had suffered

---

24   Charles Dickens, *The Life of our Lord* (Knoxville: Wordsworth Classics, 1995), 124, 127.

Death"[25]; and "they knew that if they did their duty, they would go to Heaven."[26] But as seen earlier, the only form of imitation relevant to our conversion and salvation is to take the same step of saving faith in Christ crucified as others have taken before us. Only then, indwelt by God the Holy Spirit, can we begin to imitate other Christians and even the Lord Jesus Christ Himself.

Even so, the undertaking is still a momentous one. The subject has inspired the minds of many and has been covered at length and in every conceivable detail. In 1441, a devotional book entitled, *The Imitation of Christ*, attributed to the priest, monk, and mystic Thomas à Kempis (1379/80-1471) appeared. Though an influential book and beloved by many Christian people, its readers should be aware that its writer adhered to all the false Roman doctrines exposed by the Reformers a century later. Nevertheless, as Stalker points out, the writer usually seeks Christ Himself without the interference of any other mediator.[27] C. H. Spurgeon comments

> "The Imitation of Christ"[sic] is a wonderful book upon the subject, which every Christian should read. It has its faults, but its excellencies are many. May we not only read the book, but write it out anew in our own life and character by seeking in everything

---

25   Ibid, 123.
26   Ibid, 124.
27   James Stalker, *Imago Christi: The Example of Jesus Christ* (London: Hodder & Stoughton, 1889), 17.

to be like to Jesus! It is a good thing to put up in your house the question, "What would Jesus do?" It answers nine out of ten of the difficulties of moral casuistry. When you do not know what to do, and the law does not seem very explicit on it, put it so— "What would Jesus do?"[28]

The imitation of Christ was a popular theme in nineteenth century Christian literature. In 1867, an anonymous book appeared entitled, *"Follow me," or, Jesus Our Example*, which contains a wealth of scriptural comparisons between the Savior's example and His disciples' imitation. James Stalker's *Imago Christi: The Example of Jesus Christ* considers Christ in the home, in the state, in the church, as a friend, in society, as a man of prayer, as a student of Scripture, as a worker, as a sufferer, as a philanthropist, as a winner of souls, as a preacher, as a teacher, as a controversialist, as a man of feeling, and as an influence.[29]

In 1896, adopting a totally different approach, the American preacher Charles M. Sheldon (1857-1946) grappled with the question posed by Spurgeon above ("What would Jesus do?") in his novel *In His Steps* based on 1 Peter 2:21: "For hereunto were ye called; because Christ also suffered for you, leaving you an example, that ye should follow His steps."[30] Our task in this

---

28   Charles H. Spurgeon, *Metropolitan Tabernacle Pulpit, Vol. 37, No. 2210* (London: Passmore & Alabaster, 1891), 347.

29   James Stalker, *Imago Christi: The Example of Jesus Christ* (London: Hodder & Stoughton, 1889), chapter headings.

30   Charles Sheldon, *In His Steps* (Chicago: The Advance, 1897).

chapter will be simply to limit ourselves to the examples of Christ spotlighted as such in Scripture, but the example is still a sublime one to follow.

Martyn Lloyd-Jones in his sermon on Ephesians 5:1-2 entitled "Imitators of God," makes the following comments:

> Here in this new chapter we come to what is perhaps Paul's supreme argument, to the highest level of all in doctrine and in practice, to the ultimate ideal. There is nothing possible beyond this. This is the highest statement of Christian doctrine that one can conceive of or even imagine. It is really staggering, it is almost incredible; but here it is. "Be ye followers of God"! A better translation is desirable, for the word *followers* does not bring out the meaning as it should. The Apostle really says: "Become *imitators* of God," indeed "Become *mimics* of God".[sic] Our word *mimic* comes from the very word the Apostle used. We are to mimic God, we are to imitate God. Is this possible? Is not this gross exaggeration? Has not the Apostle run away with himself, and allowed his eloquence to dazzle him? Is he seriously asking men and women like ourselves, living in a world like this, surrounded by temptations, harassed by the devil, with sin and evil and unworthiness within us, to be 'imitators of God'? Is it possible?[31]

---

31   D. Martyn Lloyd-Jones, "Imitators of God," *Darkness and Light* (Edinburgh: Banner of Truth, 1982), 291-292. Words emphasized in italics are as such in the author's original text.

Lloyd-Jones goes on (pp. 292-3) to suggest some answers to these questions; we cannot imitate God in the non-communicable attributes which are true only of Him, such as His Glory, His eternity, His majesty, His omnipotence, His omnipresence, and His omniscience. But we can seek to imitate God in His moral and communicable attributes, such as His Holiness, His righteousness, His justice, His goodness, His love, His mercy, His compassion, His tenderness, His longsuffering, His lovingkindness, His faithfulness, and His forgiveness.[32]

C. H. Spurgeon had expressed the same thoughts in another way in his own sermon, "Imitators of God," also based on Ephesians 5:1:

> We cannot imitate God in His power, or omnipresence, or omniscience; certain of his attributes are incommunicable, and of them we may say - they are high and we cannot attain to them; but these are not intended in the precept. Creatures cannot imitate their Creator in His divine attributes, but children may copy their Father in His moral attributes. By the aid of His divine Spirit we can copy our God in His justice, righteousness, holiness, purity, truth, and faithfulness. We can be tenderhearted, kind, forbearing, merciful, forgiving; in a word, we may walk in love as Christ also hath loved us.[33]

32   Ibid.
33   Charles H. Spurgeon, "Imitators of God," *Metropolitan Tabernacle Pulpit, Vol. 29, No. 1725* (London: Passmore & Alabaster, 1883), 330.

It goes without saying that any imitation of Christ must include avoiding the ungodly behavior of the unconverted. Paul warns against such ungodly behavior in Ephesians 4:17-19. "This I say, therefore, and testify in the Lord, that you should no longer walk as the rest of the Gentiles walk, in the futility of their mind, having their understanding darkened, being alienated from the life of God, because of the ignorance that is in them, because of the blindness of their heart; who, being past feeling, have given themselves over to lewdness, to work all uncleanness with greediness." The very thought of indulging in such behavior is then brushed aside with a curt, "You have not so learned Christ" (v. 20). In His death, Christ took action to put away our sin; and in the Christian life, we are to adopt and maintain the same attitude toward sin (Rom. 6:10-12; 1 Peter 4:1-3).

However, this is not the place to rehearse again the avoidance of bad examples considered earlier. Rather the imitation of Christ continues to take us in a positive direction. In another of his sermons Spurgeon stated, "You never find Christ doing a thing which you may not imitate."[34] Whether at a wedding or a funeral, on the mountain top or in the crowd, with enemies or with friends, being worshipped or despised, says Spurgeon, "Everywhere you may imitate Christ."[35] However, the imitation of Christ by no means applies to everything He did; John Calvin (1509-1564), commenting on 1 Peter 2:21, wrote:

---

34   Charles H. Spurgeon, "Christ About His Father's Business," *New Park Street Pulpit, Vol. 3, No. 122* (London: Passmore & Alabaster, 1857) pp. 123-4.
35   Ibid.

It is necessary to know what in Christ is to be our example. He walked on the sea, He cleansed the leprous, He raised the dead, He restored sight to the blind: to try to imitate Him in these things would be absurd. For when He gave these evidences of His power, it was not His object that we should thus imitate Him. It has hence happened that His fasting for forty days has been made without reason an example; but what He had in view was far otherwise. We ought, therefore, to exercise in this respect a right judgment."[36]

Three particular areas of our Lord's life are specifically highlighted in the New Testament as providing examples for us to imitate. In these, we see the examples of Christ as Servant, Sufferer, and Savior.

CHRIST AS SERVANT

As seen already, Paul's instruction—"Imitate me, just as I also imitate Christ" (1 Cor. 11:1)—was made in the context of Christian service. In particular, Paul's aim was not to please himself but to please others in the sense of seeking to be of service to them by leading them to faith in Christ (1 Cor. 10:33). He wanted the Corinthians to display the same Christlike attitude. Paul

---

36 John Calvin, *Commentaries on the Catholic Epistles* (Edinburgh: Calvin Translation Society, 1855) p. 89.

employed the same teaching in other epistles, again backed up by the example of Christ.

His message to the Romans was:

> Let each of us please his neighbor for his good, leading to edification. For even Christ did not please Himself; but as it is written, "The reproaches of those who reproached You fell on Me." For whatever things were written before were written for our learning, that we through the patience and comfort of the Scriptures might have hope. . . . Therefore receive one another, just as Christ also received us, to the glory of God. Now I say that Jesus Christ has become a servant (Rom. 15:2-4, 7-8).

The message could not be clearer: if Christ served us, Christians should serve each other. The same thought was sown in the minds of the Philippians: "Let this mind be in you which was also in Christ Jesus, who, being in the form of God, did not consider it robbery to be equal with God, but made Himself of no reputation, taking the form of a bondservant" (Phil. 2:5-7).

We have not only Paul's word for it, but we also find the sole recorded occurrence of the word "example" being on the lips of the Savior Himself. At the Lord's Supper, Jesus adopted the position of a servant and washed His disciples' feet before giving them the following explanation:

Do you know what I have done to you? You call Me Teacher and Lord, and you say well, for so I am. If I then, your Lord and Teacher, have washed your feet, you also ought to wash one another's feet. For I have given you an example, that you should do as I have done to you. Most assuredly, I say to you, a servant is not greater than his master; nor is he who is sent greater than he who sent him. If you know these things, blessed are you if you do them (John 13:12-17).

Some Christians have taken our Lord's example literally and engaged in mutual feet washing, but it is surely to be taken in a broader sense. The commentators have rightly pointed out that there is no scriptural evidence of the apostles ever obeying this instruction literally, though among the qualifications for the enrollment of a widow was that she should have "washed the saints' feet" (1 Tim. 5:10). Henry Alford, commenting on the King James Version, notes that the Lord did not command His apostles to do "that which" He had just done to them but "in like manner as" He had done.[37] It was an example, not in the sense of a specific ordinance, like baptism and the Lord's Supper but in the sense of a striking and unforgettable visual aid, illustrating humility and servanthood. What really counts is the principle rather than the specific act, the spirit rather than the letter. Bob Sheehan (1951-1997) gives as his meditation to day 182 of his *Daily Readings from J.C.*

---

37   Henry Alford, *The New Testament for English Readers* (Chicago: Moody Press reprint, n.d.), 579.

Ryle Volume Two the following telling comment: "Copying actions to the letter in a mimicking way is not as helpful as applying the principle of the action to each situation."[38]

In his commentary on this passage, Matthew Henry (1662-1714) fittingly remarks, "What a good teacher Christ is. He teaches by example as well as doctrine, and for this end came into this world, that he might set us a copy; and it is a copy without one false stroke. What good scholars we must be. We must do as he hath done; he gave us a copy, that we should write after it. Christ's example herein is to be followed by ministers in particular, in whom the graces of humility and holy love should especially appear."[39]

Jesus taught His disciples to adopt the attitude of servants and slaves (Mark 10:43-44) and underlined this aspect of His teaching by His own great example. "For even the Son of Man did not come to be served, but to serve, and to give His life a ransom for many" (v. 45). The last phrase naturally takes us forward to a consideration of His greatest act of service as the Suffering Servant.

CHRIST AS SUFFERER

The examples of faith and patience exhibited by Old Testament believers in Hebrews 11 culminate in the supreme example of our Savior who "when He suffered" in the words of Peter "committed

---

38 Robert Sheehan, *Daily Readings from J.C. Ryle Vol. 2* (Darlington: Evangelical Press, 1985).

39 Matthew Henry, *Commentary on the Whole Bible in One Volume* (London: Marshall, Morgan & Scott, 1960), 383.

Himself to Him who judges righteously" (1 Pet. 2:23). He above all others is set before us for our consideration and imitation. So the writer of Hebrews instructs his readers to look to Jesus, Who "endured the cross, despising the shame . . . consider Him who endured such hostility from sinners against Himself, lest you become weary and discouraged in your souls" (Heb. 12:2-3). Toward the end of the epistle he again takes up the suffering of Christ as an example: "Therefore Jesus also, that He might sanctify the people with His own blood, suffered outside the gate. Therefore let us go forth to Him, outside the camp, bearing His reproach" (Heb. 13:12-13).

Peter himself in his first epistle was writing to many who were likely to suffer for their Christian faith. His instruction to servants who suffered unjustly at the hands of cruel masters was to remember the example of Christ:

> When you do good and suffer, if you take it patiently, this is commendable before God. For to this you were called, because Christ also suffered for us, leaving us an example, that you should follow His steps: "Who committed no sin, nor was deceit found in His mouth"; who, when He was reviled, did not revile in return; when He suffered, He did not threaten, but committed Himself to Him who judges righteously (1 Peter 2:20-23).

In their own imitation of other believers and of the Lord, the Thessalonians had suffered "much affliction" (1 Thess. 1:6) in keeping with the words of Jesus: "If the world hates you, you know that it hated Me before it hated you . . . If they persecuted Me, they will also persecute you" (John 15:18, 20).

It is in this area in particular that the imitation of Christ has been most seriously misunderstood and misapplied. James Stalker stresses that "it is a point of the greatest practical importance to emphasize that in experience the true order is, that the imitation of Christ should follow the forgiveness of sins through the blood of His cross."[40] However, liberal theologians have been all too ready to deny the atonement by depicting our Savior's death merely as an example, either of God's love, or how to face up to suffering. As quoted above, Peter presents various aspects of our Lord's response to suffering as examples to imitate. Christ suffered unjustly without seeking vengeance and without threatening, but instead committed Himself to His loving Heavenly Father (1 Peter 2:22-23). But Peter guards against the possibility of misinterpreting this by proceeding to an explanation of the primary truth about the cross: "Who Himself bore our sins in His own body on the tree, that we, having died to sins, might live for righteousness— by whose stripes you were healed" (1 Peter 2:24).

While we can be encouraged to react to suffering in the same way as the Savior did, what His suffering achieved for us is unique, inimitable, and unrepeatable. Other examples can be similarly applied from His saving work on our behalf. We cannot

---

40   James Stalker, *Imago Christi: The Example of Jesus Christ* (London: Hodder & Stoughton, 1889), p. 26.

imitate His work as Savior, but we should imitate His attitudes as Savior.

CHRIST AS SAVIOR

Paul takes up this theme in Ephesians where there are two practical aspects of Christ's saving work for our mutual emulation, namely forgiveness and love: "And be kind to one another, tenderhearted, forgiving one another, even as God in Christ forgave you. Therefore be imitators of God as dear children. And walk in love, as Christ also has loved us and given Himself for us, an offering and a sacrifice to God for a sweet-smelling aroma" (Eph. 4:32-5:2).

If God in Christ could serve us, we should serve each other, Paul taught the Romans. Similarly, if God in Christ can forgive us, we should be able to forgive each other. Indeed, it is compulsory: "Even as Christ forgave you, so you also must do" (Col. 3:13). The Lord's indignation toward those who fail to follow His example of forgiveness is graphically illustrated in His parable of the unforgiving servant (Matt. 18:32-35).

If Christ can love us and give Himself for us, we should love each other. His words, "Therefore you shall be perfect, just as your Father in heaven is perfect" (Matt. 5:48), were spoken in the immediate context of the need to love not only those who love us, but even our enemies. God sets us the example by showering His common grace on both the evil and the good, on both the just and the unjust (Matt. 5:45). Paul proceeds to treat Christ's sacrificial love toward us not only as a general example directed at all believers but also as a specific one for husbands to copy toward their wives. The benefits also can be mutual. For example, if husbands love their wives "just as Christ also loved the church and gave Himself for her" (Eph. 5:25), it must make it easier for wives to be submissive to their husbands "as to the Lord" (Eph. 5:22); in a similar context, Sarah's obedience to her husband Abraham is commended for wives to imitate (1 Peter 3:5-6).

The same mutual application is found in John's first epistle: "By this we know love, because He laid down His life for us. And we also ought to lay down our lives for the brethren" (1 John 3:16). "In this the love of God was manifested toward us, that God has sent His only begotten Son into the world, that we might live through Him. In this is love, not that we loved God, but that He loved us and sent His Son to be the propitiation for our sins. Beloved, if God so loved us, we also ought to love one another" (1 John 4:9-11). This instruction goes right back to the words of the Savior Himself: "A new commandment I give to you, that you love one another; as I have loved you, that you also love one another" (John 13:34). "This is my commandment, that you love one another as I have loved you" (John 15:12).

The imitation of Christ is, therefore, not only a real possibility but His own commandment to us! Christians have an obligation "to walk just as He walked" (1 John 2:6). Albert Barnes exclaims, "What a simple rule this is! And how much contention would be avoided if it were followed! If every Christian who is angry, unforgiving, and unkind, would just ask himself the question, 'How does God treat me?' it would save all the trouble and heart-burning which ever exists in the church."[41] Spurgeon states, "Imitation of God is the sincerest form of admiring him"[42] and "Be like Christ, or be not called a Christian"[43]

The imitation of Christ reaches perhaps its most sublime expression in Philippians 2:5-11 in which His work as Servant, Sufferer, and Savior is wonderfully combined:

> Let this mind be in you which was also in Christ Jesus, who, being in the form of God, did not consider it robbery to be equal with God, but made Himself of no reputation, taking the form of a bondservant, and coming in the likeness of men. And being found in appearance as a man, He humbled Himself and became obedient to the point of death, even the death of the cross. Therefore God also has highly exalted Him and given Him the name which is above every name, that at the name of Jesus every knee should bow, of those in heaven, and of those on earth, and of those under the earth, and that every tongue should confess that Jesus Christ is Lord, to the glory of God the Father.

---

41 Alfred Barnes, *A Popular Family Commentary on the New Testament, Vol. 7* (London: The Gresham Publishing Company, 1868), 95.
42 Charles H. Spurgeon "Imitators of God," *Metropolitan Tabernacle Pulpit, Vol. 29, No. 1725* (London, Passmore & Alabaster 1883), 326-7.
43 Ibid, 332.

In this passage, even in His exaltation, He is an example to us of the principles by which God operates. "He humbled Himself . . . Therefore God also has highly exalted Him" (vv. 8-9). God employs the very same principles toward us: "Whoever exalts himself will be humbled, and he who humbles himself will be exalted" (Luke 14:11, c.f. Luke 18:14 and 1 Peter 5:5-6).

If the imitation of Christ still seems to be way beyond our capabilities, these commands from God should also be seen as encouragements to imitate Him. In the sermon mentioned above Spurgeon points out that being asked to imitate God is not as difficult as some of the things which God has already done for the believer, things which would have been impossible for us to do in our own strength.[44] Already, He has made us His children; He has given us His nature; He has given us His Spirit, and we actually have fellowship with Him!

These momentous facts are also aspects of vital importance. We must be God's children and united to Christ by faith in Him before our imitation of Him is either possible or of any value. Stalker points out that:

> Beautiful as the phrase "the imitation of Christ" is, it hardly indicates the deepest way in which Christ's people become like Him. Imitation is rather an external process; it denotes the taking of that which is on one and putting it on another from the outside.

---

44   Ibid.

But it is not chiefly by such an external copying that a Christian grows like Christ, but by an internal union with Him.[45]

He continues to say:

We may carefully copy the traits of Christ's character, looking at Him outside of us, as a painter looks at his model; we may do better still—we may, by prayer and the reading of the Word, live daily in His company, and receive the impress of His influence; but, if our imitation of Him is to be the deepest and most thorough, something more is necessary: He must be in us . . . having communicated His own nature to us in the new birth.[46]

---

45 James Stalker, *Imago Christi: The Example of Jesus Christ* (London: Hodder & Stoughton, 1889), 27.
46 Ibid, 28.

Chapter 7

SETTING A GOOD EXAMPLE

HAVING ADVANCED FROM EXAMPLES TO avoid to examples to follow, from the imitation of faith through the imitation of godliness, to the imitation of Christ Himself, one could be forgiven for thinking that the goal and summit of this subject has been reached. But there is a further stage to climb. The Corinthians had got stuck at the very beginning and still needed teaching on bad examples to be avoided, whereas the Thessalonians had not only advanced to the imitation of faith, godliness, and Christ but had also gone the extra mile as well. They had become examples to others on a large scale, and their example had become almost proverbial.

Paul testifies of them:

> And you became followers of us and of the Lord, having received the word in much affliction, with joy of the Holy Spirit, so that you became examples

> to all in Macedonia and Achaia who believe. For
> from you the word of the Lord has sounded forth,
> not only in Macedonia and Achaia, but also in every
> place. Your faith toward God has gone out, so that we
> do not need to say anything. (1 Thess. 1:6-8).

It is one thing to be imitators but quite another to become examples. Matthew Poole comments on 2 Thessalonians 3:9 that "it is desirable to follow good examples, but more to become a good example."[47] By imitating Christ, Paul had become an example for others to imitate, and the Thessalonians had done the same.

The Greek word used by Paul in 1 Thessalonians 1:7 is "*tupos*," from which we derive the English word "type." This same word is used to describe the "pattern" or blueprint of the tabernacle shown to Moses by God on Mount Sinai before the tabernacle's construction (Acts 7:44; Heb. 8:5). Likewise, Paul describes the Thessalonians as a pattern upon which other believers can model themselves. Daniel Mayo, the compiler of the 1 Thessalonians portion of Matthew Henry's unfinished commentary, says that the Thessalonians were like "stamps, or instruments to make impression with. They had themselves received good impressions, and they made good impressions. Christians should be so good as by their example to influence others."[48]

---

47   Matthew Poole, *A Commentary on the Holy Bible, Vol. 3* (London, Banner of Truth reprint, 1963), 769.

48   Matthew Henry, *Commentary on the Whole Bible in One Volume* (London: Marshall, Morgan & Scott, 1960), 675.

The responsibility resting upon churches and upon individual believers is an awesome one. We are either setting good examples for others to imitate as part of their growth in the faith; or we are setting bad examples, which would lead others astray and which they should, therefore, avoid like the plague. In this respect pastors, in particular, have a great responsibility.

PASTORS AND THEIR FLOCKS

Apart from the Thessalonian instance, the epistles contain three references to the setting of good examples by role-models. These are all addressed to Christian leaders and pastors; but by a simple argument, it can be proved that they are also relevant to all believers. If pastors are to exhibit qualities for their flocks to imitate, it follows that their flocks should be aiming at the very same qualities which are required of their pastors! In 1 Timothy 3:1-13 and Titus 1:5-9, qualities are listed which are essential in those considered suitable to serve as elders and deacons. But these are the same kinds of qualities which all Christians, whether young or old, male or female, should be aiming at; they, like their leaders, should seek to be, for example, sober-minded, sound in faith, and not given to wine (compare Titus 1:7-9 with 2:1-6, noting in 2:7 the role Titus' own good example was to play in promoting this).

Part of the role of church leaders is to equip the rest of the saints to play their part in the work of the ministry (Eph. 4:12). One of the means of achieving and furthering this aim is the setting of good examples. It was certainly working in Thessalonica, where good examples were being set by the whole church, not only by its leadership. No believer can justify excusing himself or herself from the responsibility of setting a good example to others.

Peter gives the following exhortation to elders: "Shepherd the flock of God which is among you, serving as overseers, not by compulsion but willingly, not for dishonest gain but eagerly; nor as being lords over those entrusted to you, but being examples to the flock; and when the Chief Shepherd appears, you will receive the crown of glory that does not fade away" (1 Peter 5:2-4). Setting good examples is the way to achieve this; some, like Diotrephes (3 John 9-11), employed the other styles of leadership mentioned by Peter, but these other methods are really worldly examples to be avoided.

To expand on this point, Christian ministry is not to be treated merely as a profession, and heavy shepherding in the form of controlling and bullying the flock finds no place there either— it belongs to the world's methods of leadership and is directly opposed to our Lord's teaching and example. He stated that "those who are considered rulers over the Gentiles lord it over them . . . Yet it shall not be so among you; but whoever desires to become great among you shall be your servant . . . For even the Son of Man did not come to be served, but to serve" (Mark 10:42-45). While we find Him described as the Chief Shepherd (1 Peter 5:4), the Good and Giving Shepherd (John 10:11) and the Great Shepherd (Heb. 13:20), Jesus is never called the Heavy Shepherd! On the contrary,

He said, "Come to Me, all you who labor and are heavy laden, and I will give you rest. Take My yoke upon you and learn from Me, for I am gentle and lowly in heart, and you will find rest for your souls. For my yoke is easy and My burden is light" (Matt. 11:28-30).

Scripture teaches Christian leaders that a good example carries far more weight and is far more effective than sheer brute force. Much the same could be said about good leadership in the family and in the workplace. "Husbands, love your wives and do not be bitter toward them . . . Fathers, do not provoke your children, lest they become discouraged . . . Masters, give your bondservants what is just and fair, knowing that you also have a Master in heaven" (Col. 3:19-4:1). The principles taught to pastors about setting a good example to their flocks are just as relevant to the individual members of the flocks as well.

THE MODEL CHRISTIAN

There are two other references to setting a good example, both found in the Pastoral Epistles. Paul's instruction to Titus is of a general nature: "In all things showing yourself to be a pattern of good works" (Titus 2:7). But the parallel instruction to Timothy goes into specific details: "Let no one despise your youth, but be an example to the believers in word, in conduct, in love, in spirit, in faith, in purity" (1 Tim. 4:12).

There are some general points of interest to note here. First, it is crystal clear that Timothy's comparative youth was no disadvantage to his setting a good example. In God's eyes a good example is neither dependent upon the experience of old age nor restricted by the inexperience of youth. Timothy's example carried far more weight than his age ever could. Indeed, ever since Paul had first met him, Timothy had been a consistently good example to others (Acts 16:1-2; 1 Cor. 4:17; Phil. 2:19-22). Paul here encourages him to go on being such. Secondly, Paul lists several examples of godly conduct, which are in sharp contrast to the examples of ungodly conduct which we have already seen listed by him in 1 Corinthians 10 for the avoidance of his readers. Whereas the Corinthians were warned against the works of the flesh, Timothy is encouraged to display the works of the Spirit in the good examples which should be set by pastors to their flocks and which should in turn be imitated and set by their flocks. We have already touched upon some of these aspects in earlier chapters, but it will be worth examining 1 Timothy 4:12 in some detail.

"In word, in conduct"—these two basic and general aspects go together and confirm each other. "Do as I say" and "do as I do" should work in harmony with each other, not in contradiction. Inappropriate conduct will nullify the finest-sounding words. As someone has said, "What you are speaks so loudly, I can't hear a word you're saying!" The story has been told of one whose preaching was so inspiring that his people wished he would never leave the pulpit but whose lifestyle was so disgraceful that they felt he should never enter the pulpit! Failure to practice what they preached was one of the faults of the Pharisees—Jesus said they should be obeyed but not imitated "for they say and do not do" (Matt. 23:3). Those who fall into the same trap set examples to be avoided. A far better model was that of Ezra in Old Testament times. He "prepared his heart to seek the Law of the LORD, and to do it, and to teach statutes and ordinances in Israel" (Ezra 7:10). The word-order suggests that his aim was not so much to practice what he preached as to be able to preach what he practiced. How many of us would dare to do that?

On the other hand, inappropriate speech can ruin the effect of the best conduct. This second aspect is amplified in Paul's instructions to Titus: "In all things showing yourself to be a pattern of good works; in doctrine showing integrity, reverence, incorruptibility, sound speech that cannot be condemned, that one who is an opponent may be ashamed, having nothing evil to say of you" (Titus 2:7-8). A pastor—or, for that matter, any Christian—whose words fall below the standard of his deeds will also invite justifiable criticism.

Martyn Lloyd-Jones refers to the famous instance of the clergyman Studdert-Kennedy, who had been an army chaplain during the First World War. Studdert-Kennedy clearly followed the principle "When in Rome, do as the Romans do," since his chosen method of reaching others was to be like them, even if that meant smoking and swearing as they did.[49] But that is to miss the point completely—according to the Scriptures the Christian

---

49   D. Martyn Lloyd-Jones, *Preaching & Preachers* (London, Hodder & Stoughton, 1971), 139-40.

minister or layman is not expected to sink to the levels of the world but to demonstrate to the world a higher and better way.

It was by the combination of his wicked behavior and evil-speaking that Diotrephes became the villain of John's third epistle and an evil example to be avoided (3 John 9-11). Ungodly behavior has no place in the life of the Christian leader; similarly crude language and rude stories have no place in the pulpit because they can be justifiably criticized and, therefore, do not qualify as "sound speech that cannot be condemned." Jeremiah Smith, who wrote the Titus portion of Matthew Henry's commentary, gives a positive slant to this point: "In their preaching, therefore, the display of human learning or oratory, is not to be affected; but sound speech must be used, which cannot be condemned; scripture-language in expressing scripture-truths. This is sound speech, that cannot be condemned."[50]

It is not only in the pulpit but in the daily life of every believer that sound speech is required. Paul makes much of this point in the fourth and fifth chapters of Ephesians. "Therefore, putting away lying, 'Let each one of you speak truth with his neighbor'" (4:25); "Let no corrupt word proceed out of your mouth, but what is good for necessary edification, that it may impart grace to the hearers" (4:29); "Let all bitterness, wrath, anger, clamor, and evil speaking be put away from you, with all malice" (4:31). Paul says that there should be "neither filthiness, nor foolish talking, nor coarse jesting, which are not fitting, but rather giving of thanks"

---

50   Henry, 700.

(5:4). The point is rammed home when we realize that it is in this very context that we are instructed to "be imitators of God as dear children" (5:1), forgiving and loving each other (4:32; 5:2).

The aim of the Christian is summed up in the book of Colossians. "And whatever you do in word and deed, do all in the name of the Lord Jesus, giving thanks to God the Father through Him" (Col. 3:17). "Walk in wisdom toward those who are outside, redeeming the time. Let your speech always be with grace, seasoned with salt, that you may know how you ought to answer each one" (Col. 4:5-6). Godly speech and godly behavior go together, and Christian leaders who are setting that kind of consistent example are the ones who are worth imitating. "Remember those who rule over you, who have spoken the word of God to you, whose faith follow, considering the outcome of their conduct" (Heb. 13:7).

"In love"—the importance of imitating Christ's example of love has already been considered in the previous chapter, but some further points may be made in this context. Paul says elsewhere that even the finest examples of speech, conduct, and faith (which appears later in 1 Tim. 4:12) come to nothing if love is absent. "Though I speak with the tongues of men and of angels, but have not love, I have become sounding brass or a clanging cymbal . . . And though I have all faith, so that I could remove mountains, but have not love, I am nothing. And though I bestow all my goods to feed the poor, and though I give my body to be burned, but have not love, it profits me nothing" (1 Cor. 13:1-3). "Above all these things put on love which is the bond of perfection"

(Col. 3:14). Peter's words are almost identical: "And above all things have fervent love for one another, for 'love will cover a multitude of sins'" (1 Peter 4:8). The Lord Jesus Christ is the great example of love which we should imitate and love is an essential example to set for others: "Let all that you do be done with love" (1 Cor. 16:14).

"In spirit"—this aspect is not in all the manuscripts and therefore does not appear in every translation, but it is an important one. It is not immediately obvious what Paul was saying. How exactly could Timothy set an example "in spirit"? The best answer may be to list the kinds of spirit which are commended in the New Testament. "Blessed are the poor in spirit" (Matt. 5:3), said the Savior. Elsewhere, we read of a "willing" spirit (Matt. 26:41), being "strong in spirit" (Luke 1:80; 2:40), rejoicing "in the Spirit" (Luke 10:21), worshipping "in spirit" (John 4:23, c.f. Phil. 3:3), being "fervent in spirit" (Acts 18:25; Rom. 12:11), "a spirit of gentleness" (1 Cor. 4:21; Gal. 6:1), "the spirit of wisdom" (Eph. 1:17), a spirit "of power and of love and of a sound mind" (2 Tim. 1:7), and finally, "a gentle and quiet spirit" (1 Pet. 3:4). When these are all combined, the result is surely a good example of someone "filled with the Holy Spirit," a condition which was exhibited corporately by the early church (Acts 4:31), required of those in Christian leadership (Acts 6:3, 5; 11:22-24), and commanded to all believers (Eph. 5:18). The model Christian is one who displays the fruit of the Spirit (Gal. 5:22-23).

"In faith"—it has already been demonstrated at length how large a part the topic of faith plays in the matter of teaching by examples in the New Testament. Timothy had himself followed the example of saving faith set by his grandmother Lois and his mother Eunice (2 Tim. 1:5). In 1 Timothy 4:6, Paul encouraged Timothy to continue his imitation of faith by being "a good minister of Jesus Christ, nourished in the words of faith." Six verses later, Timothy is instructed to advance to the next stage— that is, by being an example of faith for others to imitate. No doubt, he was to be an example of saving faith to those who needed to believe; but in the immediate context, he was also to be an example to other Christians of ongoing faith working itself out in his life. Among other things, the man of God is to have faith as his aim (1 Tim. 6:11; 2 Tim. 2:22) and to "fight the good fight of faith" (1 Tim. 6:12). Christian leaders should demonstrate to their flocks a faith worth imitating (Heb. 13:7).

"In purity" Jesus said, "Blessed are the pure in heart, for they shall see God" (Matt. 5:8). In his two letters to Timothy, Paul demonstrated the vital connection between purity and some of the other graces we have already considered in this list. Inward purity is one of the roots of true love: "Now the purpose of the commandment is love from a pure heart, from a good conscience, and from sincere faith" (1 Tim. 1:5). True faith also springs from purity: "Flee also youthful lusts; but pursue righteousness, faith, love, peace with those who call on the Lord out of a pure heart" (2 Tim. 2:22). Timothy was to be an example of purity to other Christians; Paul's command to him was short and sweet: "Keep yourself pure" (1 Tim. 5:22). Nothing could be further from the worldly idea that someone can be a valuable public servant, despite being immoral in private! James typically adds his practical touch to illustrate the out-workings of purity: "Pure and undefiled religion before God and the Father is this: to visit orphans and widows in their trouble, and to keep oneself unspotted from the world" (James 1:27). What a blessing we can be to others if we set them good and consistent examples "in word, in conduct, in love, in spirit, in faith, in purity."

Chapter 8
AN OLD TESTAMENT EPILOGUE: THE EPISTLE OF JEHORAM'S LIFE

THE NEW TESTAMENT EPISTLES PROVIDE us with detailed teaching on the examples which Christians should imitate and set for others. This is clearly one of the means of grace by which the Christian can and should advance in the Christian life. Some serious questions arise. Can we afford to ignore the practice of imitation? What happens if we fail to apply its teaching? Does it really matter? To answer these questions, we need to go back to the Old Testament and to a dreadful warning of the consequences awaiting those who fail to move in the right direction and who instead continue in the wrong direction. The texts of letters are not very common in the Old Testament, but there is one preserved in 2 Chronicles 21:12-15—the text of a letter received by Jehoram, king of Judah—short, but hardly sweet:

> And a letter came to him from Elijah the prophet,
> saying, Thus says the LORD God of your father
> David: Because you have not walked in the ways of
> Jehoshaphat your father, or in the ways of Asa king of
> Judah, but have walked in the way of the kings of Israel,
> and have made Judah and the inhabitants of Jerusalem
> to play the harlot like the harlotry of the house of
> Ahab, and also have killed your brothers, those of your
> father's household, who were better than yourself,
> behold the LORD will strike your people with a
> serious affliction—your children, your wives, and all
> your possessions; and you will become very sick with
> a disease of your intestines, until your intestines come
> out by reason of the sickness, day by day.

Most recipients of such a letter would describe it either as hate-mail or as a poison pen-letter. But it was actually a letter from God, written by the hand of His inspired prophet Elijah. Interestingly enough, it would appear that Elijah was no longer on earth; it had been during the reign of the previous king of Judah, Jehoram's late father, Jehoshaphat, that Elijah had ascended to Heaven in a chariot of fire and had been succeeded as prophet by Elisha (2 Kings 3:11; 2 Chron. 21:1). It was not strictly speaking a posthumous letter because Elijah had not actually suffered death; so it would not be strictly accurate to say that he, like Abel (Heb. 11:4), was still speaking, though dead. One can only imagine Jehoram's shock upon receiving such a missive from someone who had apparently vanished into thin air some time earlier! The manner of this letter's delivery is not revealed to us, but it carried Heaven's postmark. Even more of a shock to Jehoram must have been to receive in his post such a strongly worded document which had as its theme, "Jehoram, king of Judah, This is your life." The main cause of Jehoram's imminent downfall was that he was at fault in the two basic areas we have been considering—imitation and influence.

THE WRONG KIND OF IMITATION

Jehoram had very little excuse for his wicked behavior; from his early days, he had been surrounded by good examples to imitate. The chronology of his life paints a telling picture. He became king at the age of thirty-two (2 Chron. 21:20); his father, Jehoshaphat, had been king of Judah for twenty-five of those thirty-two years (20:31). Jehoram was therefore already seven years old when his grandfather, Asa, died. While Asa and Jehoshaphat had displayed certain glaring weaknesses and failings, they had been basically godly kings who had walked in the ways of the Lord. On the whole, "Asa did what was good and right in the eyes of the LORD his God" (14:2). Jehoshaphat had walked in the ways of David and those of the Lord (17:3-6)—as well as those of his father, Asa (20:32)—while seeking to avoid the wicked ways followed by the rulers of the northern kingdom of Israel.

However, compromise was one of Jehoshaphat's weak spots. Twice, he joined forces with the wicked kings of Israel, not only injuring but also insulting himself in the process by professing to them, "I am as you are" (18:3, c.f. 2 Kings 3:7)! Jehoshaphat is a warning to any believer who disregards the doctrine of separation. He must also carry his share of the blame for sowing the seeds of future trouble by making a marriage alliance with Ahab, one of the most wicked of the kings of Israel (18:1). His oldest son, Jehoram, was thus married to Ahab's daughter (21:6) with the result that he ignored all the good examples which had surrounded him since his birth. Two generations of godly examples failed to produce godliness in him, a fact which cuts across all the superficial arguments of those who claim a spurious second-hand godliness based on being born in a Christian family or in a "Christian" country. Godly examples can get ignored because human nature is basically sinful; good examples are nowhere near as easy to apply as bad examples.

Having rejected the ways of the Lord and those of his godly father and grandfather, Jehoram had instead copied the wicked ways of the kings of Israel and, specifically, the particularly wicked ways of his father-in-law, King Ahab (21:6). His six younger brothers (named in 21:2), whom God described in the letter as having been better than Jehoram, had been murdered by Jehoram (21:4). The story could not have stopped at that point; as we have seen previously, the examples we imitate determine the nature of the examples we set for others to follow. Jehoram was to prove that the wrong kind of imitation automatically results in the wrong kind of influence.

THE WRONG KIND OF INFLUENCE

Jehoram's influence upon his subjects and his nation was devastating. By his wicked example, he led them astray into unfaithfulness, far away from the ways of God (2 Chron. 21:11). The Lord judged him and them for it. In accordance with the prophecy with which Elijah's letter ended, Jehoram suffered national and personal disaster. First came invasion by hostile forces (21:16, 17); then incurable illness leading to a painful death (21:18, 19); and finally, as if to add triple insult to injury, three posthumous snubs from his people—they made no fire in his honor; no one regretted his departure; and he was denied burial in the royal tombs (21:19, 20). After his death, his son, Ahaziah, and his widow, Athaliah, carried on in his wicked ways (22:1-4); both of them would also come to violent ends (22:9; 23:15).

The story of Jehoram should be a warning to us all. When professing Christians and Christian churches imitate the wrong examples and in so doing set bad examples to follow, the Lord still takes notice of them. He has told us how to influence others for good, "Let your light so shine before men, that they may see your good works and glorify your Father in heaven" (Matt. 5:16). If our deeds do not match up to our profession, others will be influenced in the wrong direction. That principle was taught by the apostle Paul in addressing the Jews in Romans 2:21-24:

> You, therefore, who teach another, do you not teach yourself? You who preach that a man should not steal, do you steal? You who say, "Do not commit adultery," do you commit adultery? You who abhor idols, do you rob temples? You who make your boast in the law, do you dishonor God through breaking the law? For "the name of God is blasphemed among the Gentiles because of you," as it is written.

If we are tempted to treat this subject lightly, we need to hear again our Lord's words concerning those who are a bad influence upon others: "But whoever causes one of these little ones who believe in Me to sin, it would be better for him if a millstone were hung around his neck, and he were drowned in the depth of the sea. Woe to the world because of offenses! For offenses must come, but woe to that man by whom the offense comes!" (Matt. 18:6-7). The Christian is responsible before God to set examples which do not lead others astray; this factor needs to be balanced against the great freedom which broadminded believers claim as their right.

To illustrate this by one particular subject, it is easy enough to find sad incidents which point to the danger of being seen drinking alcohol or being known as a drinker of alcohol. While the one setting the example may escape without any apparent personal damage, the one following the example may end up with disastrous consequences. Others are left trying to pick up the pieces, which sometimes, like Humpty Dumpty, cannot be put back together again.

Paul addressed this principle in his letters to the Romans and Corinthians and also warned of the damage which could be done to others.

> Yet if your brother is grieved because of your food, you are no longer walking in love. Do not destroy with your food the one for whom Christ died . . . Do not destroy the work of God for the sake of food. All things indeed are pure, but it is evil for the man who eats with offense. It is good neither to eat meat nor drink wine nor do anything by which your brother stumbles or is offended or is made weak (Rom. 14:15, 20-21, c.f. 1 Cor. 8:9-13).

It was to those who boasted of their freedom to eat food publicly, which had been offered to idols that Paul wrote:

> All things are lawful for me, but not all things are helpful; all things are lawful for me, but not all things edify. Let no one seek his own, but each one the other's well-being. . . . Therefore, whether you eat or drink, or whatever you do, do all to the glory of God. Give no offense, either to the Jews or to the Greeks or to the church of God, just as I also please all men in all things, not seeking my own profit, but the profit of many, that they may be saved. Imitate me, just as I also imitate Christ (1 Corinthians 10:23-11:1).

If indulgence can be a powerful influence for evil, abstinence can be just as powerful an influence for good. This was strikingly illustrated in the strange conversion of Rees Prichard, the early seventeenth-century Vicar of Llandovery, as related by John Bulmer:

> When Mr. Prichard first came to reside at Llandovery, he was far from being qualified, in respect of personal religion, for the duties he had to perform. According to tradition he was . . . addicted to drinking. His reformation is said to have been effected in the following very singular manner. He had a favourite goat, which used to ramble about the town, and was once enticed into a public house by some loose fellows, who made it drunk with ale. After this the animal seemed more disposed than its owner, to learn wisdom from past misfortune, as it would neither come near the tavern, be induced to drink ale again, or even to endure the smell of that which had proved so hurtful and inconvenient. This sagacious conduct of his goat so powerfully arrested the mind of Mr. Prichard, as to render him ashamed of the odious sin of drunkenness, while it led to a train of reflections which, under God, became the means of his conversion! He therefore immediately entered on a more serious discharge of his ministerial duties; called the attention of his countrymen to the great doctrines of the gospel; exhorted sinners to repentance; and was very much in the habit of improving any national calamity, or

more local dispensation of providence, with a view to promote true religion.[51]

If the behavior of a goat can exert such an influence, how much more should a godly Christian, setting the best kinds of examples, be able to point others in the right direction?

THE EPISTLE OF YOUR LIFE

It is the duty of every professing believer and every Christian church to examine the example he, she, or it is setting for others. Paul described the Corinthian church in this way: "You are our epistle written in our hearts, known and read by all men" (2 Cor. 3:2). In this sense, the individual life of every believer and the corporate life of every church are like a living letter influencing others for better or worse.

C. H. Spurgeon put this thought in these terms: "A Christian should be a striking likeness of Jesus Christ, beautifully and eloquently written; but the best life of Christ is His living biography, written out in the words and actions of His people."[52]

We should all be asking ourselves the following kinds of questions—"Does my life show to others that I am truly trusting and following the Lord Jesus Christ? Is my example a good one

51   John Bulmer, *Beauties of the Vicar of Llandovery or Light from the Welshman's Candle* (London: Holdsworth and Ball, 1830), pp. iv-v.
52   Charles H. Spurgeon, *Morning by Morning* (London: Passmore & Alabaster, 1865), 42.

pointing unbelievers to faith in Him, or is it a hypocritical one driving them away from Him? Does my example build up my fellow-believers, or lead them astray into error?"

The Christian who is heading in the right direction is the one who avoids following bad examples; who practices the imitation of faith, the imitation of godliness, and the imitation of Christ; and who, in so doing, sets good examples for others to follow. Paul's instruction is "that you put off, concerning your former conduct, the old man which grows corrupt according to the deceitful lusts, and be renewed in the spirit of your mind, and that you put on the new man which was created according to God, in true righteousness and holiness" (Eph. 4:22-24). Or, to put it more bluntly:

"Depart from evil and do good" (Psalm 34:14; 37:27).
"Cease to do evil, Learn to do good" (Isa. 1:16-17).
"Abhor what is evil. Cling to what is good" (Rom. 12:9).
"Beloved, do not imitate what is evil, but what is good" (3 John 11).

BIBLIOGRAPHY

Alford, Henry. *The New Testament for English Readers*. Chicago: Moody Press reprint, n.d.

Barnes, Alfred. *A Popular Family Commentary on the New Testament*. London: The Gresham Publishing Company, 1868.

Bulmer, John. *Beauties of the Vicar of Llandovery or Light from the Welshman's Candle*. London: Holdsworth and Ball, 1830.

Boettner, Loraine. *Roman Catholicism*. London: Banner of Truth, 1966.

Calvin, John. *Commentaries on the Catholic Epistles*. Edinburgh: Calvin Translation Society, 1855.

Crosby, Terence. *Exemplum and Documentum in Livy*. PhD Thesis. London: King's College, University of London, 1979.

Crosby, Terence. *Opening Up 2 & 3 John*. Leominster: Day One Publications, 2006.

Dickens, Charles. *The Life of Our Lord*. Ware: Wordsworth Classics, 1995.

"Follow Me" or Jesus Our Example. London: Morgan & Chase, 1867.

Henry, Matthew. *Commentary on the Whole Bible in One Volume*. London: Marshall, Morgan & Scott, 1960.

Hodge, Charles. *A Commentary on the First Epistle to the Corinthians*. London: Banner of Truth reprint, 1958.

Josephus, Flavius. *The Works of Flavius Josephus*. Translated by William Whiston. London: James S. Virtue, n.d.

Kempis, Thomas A. *The Imitation of Christ*. Translated by C. Bigg. London: Methuen & Co., 1898.

Livius, Titus. *The Complete Livy: The History of Rome "Ab Urbe Condita."* www.bybliotech.org, 2012. Kindle.

Lloyd-Jones, D. Martyn. *Darkness and Light: An Exposition of Ephesians 4:17 to 5:17*. Edinburgh: Banner of Truth, 1982.

Lloyd-Jones, D. Martyn. *Preaching & Preachers*. London: Hodder & Stoughton, 1971.

Lloyd-Jones, D. Martyn. *Romans: An Exposition of Chapter 6: The New Man*. London: Banner of Truth, 1972.

Maximus, *Valerius. Factorum et dictorum memorabilium libri novem* (Classic reprint). London: Forgotten Books, 2019.

Owen, John. *Exposition of the Epistle to the Hebrews. An Abridgement by M. J. Tryon*. London: E. Wilmhurst, n.d.

Poole, Matthew. *A Commentary on the Holy Bible.* London: Banner of Truth reprint, 1963.

Sheehan, Robert. *Daily Readings from J. C. Ryle, Vol. 2.* Darlington: Evangelical Press, 1985.

Sheldon, Charles. *In His Steps.* Chicago: The Advance, 1897.

Spurgeon, Charles H. "The Agreement of Salvation by Grace with Walking in Good Works." *Metropolitan Tabernacle Pulpit,* Vol. 37, No. 2210. London: Passmore & Alabaster, 1891.

Spurgeon, Charles H. "Christ About His Father's business." *New Park Street Pulpit.* Vol. 3. No. 122. London: Passmore & Alabaster, 1857.

Spurgeon, Charles H. "The Form of Sound Words." *New Park Street Pulpit.* Vol. 2 No. 79. London: Passmore & Alabaster, 1856.

Spurgeon, Charles H. "Imitators of God." *Metropolitan Tabernacle Pulpit.* Vol. 29. No. 1725. London: Passmore & Alabaster, 1883.

Spurgeon, Charles H. *Morning by Morning.* London: Passmore & Alabaster, 1865.

Spurgeon, Charles H. "Portraits of Christ." *New Park Street Pulpit.* Vol.7. No.355. London: Passmore & Alabaster, 1861.

Stalker, James. *Imago Christi: The Example of Jesus Christ.* London: Hodder & Stoughton, 1889.

Tacitus, Cornelius. *Annals and Histories: Tacitus*. London: Everyman, 2012.

Thomas, Isaac. *A Puritan Golden Treasury*. Edinburgh: Banner of Truth, 1977.

Usher, Stephen. *The Historians of Greece and Rome*. London: Methuen & Co, 1970.

ABOUT THE AUTHOR

TERENCE CROSBY HOLDS A PHD in classics (Greek and Latin) from the University of London and was for some time secretary of the Evangelical Library, London. Dr. Crosby is the compiler of Day One's volumes of daily readings, *365 Days with Spurgeon* and their *C. H. Spurgeon's Forgotten* series and is the author of *Opening Up 2 and 3 John, My Book of Hobbies and God's Book, the Bible* and of *Greek to the Rescue,* the latter published by Quinta Press.

Ambassador International's mission is to magnify the Lord Jesus Christ and promote His Gospel through the written word.

We believe through the publication of Christian literature, Jesus Christ and His Word will be exalted, believers will be strengthened in their walk with Him, and the lost will be directed to Jesus Christ as the only way of salvation.

For more information about
AMBASSADOR INTERNATIONAL
please visit:

www.ambassador-international.com
@AmbassadorIntl
www.facebook.com/AmbassadorIntl

Thank you for reading this book!

You make it possible for us to fulfill our mission, and we are grateful for your partnership.

To help further our mission, please consider leaving us a review on your social media, favorite retailer's website, Goodreads or Bookbub, or our website.

Like a chef who seasons the meal in such a way that the distinctive flavors of each element is enhanced, Brian Onken invites readers of *More Than a Clever Story* into an invigorating and fresh taste of what Jesus says in His parables. Reading each parable attentive to Jesus' own words and the context in which these stories are found, you'll hear the voice of the Savior in renewed ways. No longer will you think of His parables as clever stories, but you'll find them to be life-giving words from Jesus.

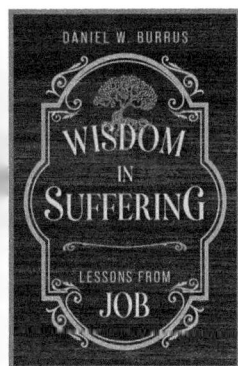

Job is a well-known name, but a deep dive into this portion of God's Word brings truth to light in a way that will illuminate our path when suffering makes life seem dark. Pain and uncertainty do not have to bring us to a place of doubt. Instead, they can be tools in the hands of a wise and loving God to draw us closer to Himself and transform our lives as we learn to trust Him and rely on His wisdom.

Most of us know Who Jesus is and would admit He was a good and kind Teacher while here on earth. But He is so much more—He is our Savior and God and worthy of all our worship. Through an in-depth study into the book of Hebrews, Joshua West and Gary Wilkerson take apart each verse, drawing the reader to a closer look at the Man Who lived here on earth for a short time and then became our Sacrifice to save us from our sins and live with us eternally in Heaven with Him. If you are searching for something more from God, dive into this study and drink in the jaw-dropping beauty of our Jesus.

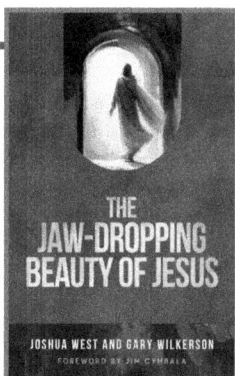

www.ingramcontent.com/pod-product-compliance
Lightning Source LLC
Chambersburg PA
CBHW071819090426
42737CB00012B/2141